New & Selected Poems
1975–2005

Howard – I enjoyed your poetry very much last month!

B.L.

First printing   2007

Acknowledgements

"The Listener" and "Ken is practicing a song" in Poetry East,
Number 15, Fall 1984, ed. Richard Jones and Kate Daniels.
"Absolutely Smooth Mustard" and "To Eat a Continent Is Not
So Strange" in Barnwood, II: 3, Spring 1983.

Library of Congress Cataloging-in Publication Data

Ronnow, Robert.
  [Poems. Selections]
  New & selected poems : 1975-2005 / by Robert Ronnow.
      p. cm.
  ISBN 978-0-935306-52-1 (alk. paper)
  I. Title. II. Title: New and selected poems.

  PS3568.O575A6 2007
  811'.54--dc22

Front cover: collage by Robert Ronnow
Book and cover design by Steve Farkas (farkasart.com)

Robert Ronnow   The Barnwood Press
168 Thornliebank Road   4604 47th Ave South
Williamstown MA 01267   Seattle WA 98118-1824
ronnow@taconic.net   www.barnwoodpress.org
www.ronnowpoetry.com

Printed in Ohio by Patterson-Britton Printing, Inc.

New & Selected Poems / 1975-2005
Robert Ronnow

Barnwood / Seattle / 2007

Contents

Brother Death   51

Belonging to the Loved Ones   115

Janie Huzzie Bows

Janie Huzzie Bows

this girl. Name her Janie Huzzie.
stalks pounding mad away from group games
complaining awkwardly loud about
her solely lonely bed always upstairs.

everybody looks. Janie Huzzie's dressed in white.
naturally the crowd glowers i pipe up
winking in every direction i slither away
mostly virtuously.

finding her. Janie Huzzie's dancing without a sound.
wherever the music's coming from
i dance a gay rubbery legged dance around
her thick stiff steps.

finally noticeable. Janie Huzzie opens her eyes.
finding herself and myself together transported
by dancing no doubt upstairs her room's filled
with one black chair (no one knows why it's there).

diplomatic and gradually. Janie Huzzie thinks she i love her.
first untouchingly then much touching day
wears into night at night i hold her
closely, soully upon her bed.

downstairs. (Janie and i hold each other sleepily.)
the crowd is waking up aiming their eyes
upstairs toward the sky
yelling jealousies.

some stories end sad or bad. Janie Huzzie's does.
daylight, crowds demanding, The Queen bursts in
sitting in the only chair smiles says
She loves me, wants me, needs me . . . takes me, too.

Mirrors

i like to dress for an imaginary girl
(we will meet each other soon) by putting on
a silk tie with subtle Chinese birds
sewn in.
she may be picturing me in her mirror
as she applies exactly the necessary line
of mascara to lengthen her lashes and darken
her eyes.
whatever begins as a mystery ends as a
blind, the nuances so well known
that birds chirp violently at their mirror images
but the pools
as they are revealed in the sunlight of
every accidental nod of the eyes remain
calm as a mirror in which there is no
image ever seen.

This looks like jump to me

You are a cockroach

you are a big cockroach crawling up a pegboard
the kitchen light suddenly shines
and you must get through to the other side
but testing every evenly spaced hole you find
your shoulders will never fit
and to get away you've got to fall.

                                    fall
or refuse to crawl and wait motionless
until inspiration with an overview filters through
or you die of hunger, lack of love, fear of death
or the outlandish hands of another angry animal
with a wisdom wiser
but infinitely useless as your own.

so you die. but now the big hands are gentle
and you receive a respite of thoughtlessness
and the garbage grave has warm chicken bones
and you don't care what happens to you
or the oldest species of proud recalcitrant insects
or procreating it or foraging a grubby kitchen sink

for food. the joy of making life is new. let go,
and through the night be carried carelessly along.

thesis: strength endures

thesis: strength endures voids and emptiness.
strength constructs no homes (antithesis:

if your house leaks then on swollen days
in sullen seasons there is no home for you)

there is endless repetitious women's strength
enduring endlessly there is this paradox:
strength is the void endured and consequently

synthesis: enter everybody's anti-hero cross-eyed,
sees crossed eyes cross-eyed but looking in his eyes
sees straight, sees sick, sees something monstrous
something insect, sees this philosophic frippery:
that is sees man

endures in his mirror that is self-doubt,
his left arm being his right arm
his left eye sees his right eye
and no eye sees his nose right.

synthesis: enter the nigger the hero's fists blazing
won't put up with that mirror is laughing
smashing his left hand smashing his right hand
naturally breaks–

enter the dumb smile of blissful blindness or
dumb sadness belting down a drink
enter an angel's colorful rags and bells
enter a man in colorful sights and smells
enter blonde beauty dragging a bulging jock.

there is the entrance where they enter through
the black hole with crescent thin edges
the animal den the fish smell the ocean motion
there is women's strength endures the stretch
the forty-eight hours of warm pain
two hours of sharp pain around mid-night
last sight the tippy-toppy veins of its head
bled and blood and body and push push Push–

and the tide goes out,
enter sleep.

Ken is practicing a song

Ken is practicing a song on the piano. Maybe he should sing it. It's a matter of course of knowing his piano. He's not practicing a song, he's practicing the piano!

I'm drinking apple juice with dextrose (a type of sugar found naturally in apples and other foods). Introducing Dextrose! Pray to Allah and maybe he will spare you when he sets the world on fire.

Where or with who will I be on that day? And how many people and adventures will I find in the wind storm and rubble? I will live, but will it matter whether or not I help anyone else to live? This is no Last Judgment. Those who have learned or who still know how to live will survive. Nobody will go to hell, they will just die. There is no limbo either. Anyone who didn't find a way to be immortal is just dead.

Striving for immortality, some Spanish philosopher (who looks like Don Quixote) says he understands and it's alright. I will read what he wrote and probably agree, but is he immortal? Not his body, but his thoughts. True, I say, but this also: Not his mind, but his thoughts. Unchanging and finite. Put them in a hatbox and pass them on as heirlooms.

Be a firm believer in dead men passing on their knowledge in print and painting. But beware of liars, don't believe everything you read. Imagine it's a friend telling you something.

Back here, I'm so afraid I can't go out by myself. It's sunset and I've been indoors all day, and inside of me is my ball of fear. We are both occupied, Ken playing the piano just burped. I'm reporting it to you. There's no good reason for you to want to know this but I am not the one meant to decide. I speak and your responsibility is to respond, and you speak and then, if I weren't going bye-bye, I'd respond to you. If you think about it, it's very hard to play a song.

The Listener

New York City is where people who are
disappearing go. It is very quiet
here, silent. A man and woman
made love below me. I could hear
the bedsprings ringing and the
woman singing in sensual pain.
My thoughts sped up as they humped
faster. Everything is dead in my room
except me and my plants. If I keep
on identifying my feelings with the
feelings of things, I too will be dead.
They are talking and laughing now. His deep
voice vibrates the air. Her laugh
is like water.

Something

Something created. Does the creator think ahead
or spill a storm. Rain happens. We supply the
reasons. Evaporation of water collecting over
huge expanses, condensed and pushed as clouds
over the land. We say it makes us sad or depressed.
We want to cry.

You describe the America you know and if you
are ashamed of yourself for what you see, you lie.
Or don't look. Loud noises of automobiles and
fumes. Today in Riverside Park, leaning on a rail,
the dead leaves and snow reminded me how far
from nature and life I am. The snow blew
in from the west. People passed in a smooth
slow line in front of me. Dogs trailing one
another. People hiding until crises bring them
out. Their dog smells another dog between the legs.
The master runs over to stop him. Maybe he
thinks they're going to fight. Doesn't want his
big German shepherd to hurt her dachshund.

Guy runs past in gray sweats on his tip-toes.
Glances at me. Another passes in blue sweats. Looks
longer. They think I'm a mugger. They are not
sexually attracted. I'm an opponent. I want something
they have. I look surly. Why aren't I out
running, disciplining myself, making myself healthy,
doing something. What brings you out here. You're not
doing anything but watching us and staring at the ground.

Walking down Broadway I realized I've never lived here and still
don't. Two women window shopping is strange to me. They talk about
the clothes. They are friends. I slow down, I don't feel so cold. Stroll,
looking at people is like a sunny day and it's a carnival. Streets different
in different weather. Rainy nights are good. Cold rainy nights. Bars filled
and warm. Streets empty and cold. People pass and look as members of
a fraternity. They need someone and don't hide it. They will try anyone
out for one night. They have tea together. They go for a drink in some
neutral place. They go straight to bed in the dark. They can't see the face.

Zach Sklar's Dream

A man and a woman are living
in a jungle. The man has lived there
all his life but the woman is new
so she's scared. The jungle is full
of snapping turtles and they are hunting some.
The man knows how to hunt them
and he kills a huge one. They drag it home
and leave it on a wooden table
in a clearing overnight. He says to the woman
Tomorrow you will clean it and cook it
in a soup. This
will accustom her to turtles
and make her less afraid.

The next morning they wake up.
But when they go into the clearing
the turtle is gone
and there's a trail of blood
leading into the jungle.
The woman panics with terror
but the man is no longer
concerned with that: he grabs
his weapons and follows
the blood into the forest.

Robinson Jeffers

Robinson Jeffers lay down on top of a mountain in a clearing (it was a sunny day)
Motionless
Watched the bald red-headed vulture sink in circles blinded by the sun
    sniffing for death
Saw the beautiful bird spread its wings to land
Sat up made the silent speech to scare him off: these bones still move,
    these lungs still breathe, this brain still labors with ideas,
These eyes still seed.

In the night when it's dark I can think.
I think the blue sky and these days made powerful by the sun's clear eye
    and a full moon
The air blown north up the river yesterday from out of the south from
    out of the ocean from out of the earth's gray unceasing mind
Were caused by me
That laying low against a hill and feeling the blind wind searching and
    missing
Is good to practice.

Ducks were playing in the sky on Wednesday
Racing in formation slung up the river by a south wind.
Sea gulls were strangely scarce even around the sewage outlets
The sun shed a ray across the water toward every lover who longed to look
And the wind in its blind unhurried search smashed a stalk of grass against a tree
Until it died.

A catalogue of all of a few things: the city
Under the influence of this full moon is unbearable at night
People stumble and kick each other impatiently, accidentally
California
Ocean, redwoods, men, women owned by men, strands of muscle
Physiology, the body, desire, a fat woman, her hairy legs and strong
    smelling queynt and flabby breasts.

A woman who calls it a queynt without pride, defiance or looking away
A man who loves to go swimming up the middle of her legs, swim
    immersed in her strong tidal swell

Shake themselves dry
Walk naked like animals climbing from rock to rock
Gripping the wet rocks, gathering berries
To eat before dusk.

Dusk, the sun sinks golden behind a palisade of cliffs
Peter notices the line of gray night that precedes all the colours
Staining cliffs mountains volcanoes plains prairies ocean forest, freedom,
    free thought, love, bodily love, bodily love, lust, last breath, life
There is nothing you can say
The trees, their colours are changing
You watch from the top of a mountain. The eye wanders to a hawk
    circling in the light.

Peter has gotten a new job

Peter has gotten a new job
as a bookstore clerk from one to ten
down by the river
in a sunny little house.
I've come to visit and I'm thumbing through
a book of poems
by Robinson Jeffers' brother.
Incoherent but
more interesting than this.

Out of the river rises a bum of a blob
dripping with water and begging a yen.
While he shivers
I call him a louse
and say This isn't Nippon, you!
So off he roams
probably back to his mother.
He was a nut
because he wasn't a fish.

Earth

Two people cannot see the same way but they can teach
One another their ways. One gives up body and soul
To follow the flow of the historical woman until
He can close his eyes and glide through mountains effortlessly.
He gives up earth and he gives up air, he gives up being touched
But he forgets to give up desiring to be touched. Then
One day the sun is hot or the moon is full, he desires
Uncontrollably to be touched and he flies smack
Into the mountain and never comes out the other side.

You live to prepare yourself to die. You leave behind
A wreck of strewn projects or a few icy pearls.
Incredibly you leave your voice behind saying
Over and over again the same words. You leave
Memories of yourself behind as pictures in the heads
Of people who wish you weren't dead or hadn't been alive.
They wash the pictorial body, shave it, comb your hair
The way they liked it best, cut a little here, add a little there,
Then easily, easily and kindly forget you.

Two hundred years later the wall crumbled and burned.
The ashes were spread logically across the plain,
A mathematical formula could describe the distribution.
The ashes were like seeds and from them
A thousand higher walls were made. It was lovely
To see those walls breathing imperceptibly
Shifting their glances so slowly as to go unnoticed
Behaving as if they were dead.

If I breathe, they breathe. If they are ash, so am I.
Having tried to separate myself and failed
I donate my body to science. The wall needs me
To breathe and hear. It gets my ears and lungs.
Trees need me to cast their night spells.
Are they asleep or are they dancing
A primitive fertility dance in the forest?
I choose trees because they can watch everything
From the distance of longevity.
To them I donate my soul.

Everything should be made of earth.
Earthen walls, earthen homes, earthen bodies, earthen sex.
Nothing should be made of air. Earth should inhale
And exhale air. Air should whip and caress earth.
Air should dry it out and crumble it. Earth.
Water should wet it and dissolve it. Earth.
What is the function of fire? Fire makes earth permanent
And then fire makes earth into air. Water
Makes earth into mud. Mud makes earth into homes.
Homes make earth into walls. Walls make the earth breathe.
Breathing makes the earth crumble. Crumbling
Makes the earth seed.

My Big Bones

Time is passing very slowly this morning while I wait for the banks to open.
A low gray cloud daubs the island north to south and muffles the trucks.
The first cool breeze since summer suddenly began squeezes in through
    the open window.
An old lover with her changed body is returned and failed to notice how
    my spirit is changed and straight as a hexagram.

This sadness like a black kid throwing a sharp rock at someone he
    doesn't know,
A vigorous breeze rummaging the tops of trees with its cool passion
    before the storm,
Sailors in a dream gripping ropes and swinging in the maelstrom fits,
And I would like to remove it like tight clothing.

The river calls the drunks who have truly dropped dead to sprawl at her side
While nearby a large Spanish family with its mother's pretty daughters
    picnics on Saturday
And the stray that lives on water rats sneaks by hugging the railroad tracks.
I mention these not as contrasts. The same river eventually seduces us all.

To continue, because the banks open in fifteen minutes.
Like a four year old watching a steam roller pave a new suburban street
Or the involuntary voyeur who cannot tell if he's her rapist or her lover,
My big bones.

A Yellow Rose

I am thinking of the day
        I came to you
                with a yellow rose

a passing businessman
        said hello to you
                you put it in your hair

today is like that day
        the sun is hot
                on a crowded city

we are discovering each other
        anew
                in the crowd

Love

When my grandfather died, my grandmother
Offered to open the coffin but I declined to
Look. Here is this hollow space on the earth
I occupy. People neither visit or not visit. Far away
Their thoughts wriggle like sperm through the universe
To my oval mind. The intensity of the confusion in the air
Around it causes them to despair. Our friendships
Dissolve. Old lovers cry a little, learn my lesson,
Face their lives alone.

I ask the pond where I can find such
Clarity and calm. A bullfrog yawns
As though nothing mattered but love.
I look over my shoulder and a tall woman
Has been following me through the morning mists.
Among songs of orioles we climb a high rock
And dangle our legs. Where
We'd expected the ocean was the still pond where
Bullfrogs ceased their mating croaks only at mid-day.
We arrived early in the morning. The mists were heavy
And the sun gradually burned them away.

There is love in the land. Some claim
It is one love that's certain. There are my friends
The wandering Jews, their love of humanity and
Ideas. Fickle as the one and ephemeral as the other
These seem even surer. There is love
Of a woman, her substantial flesh, its sweat
And cycles, the two of you bitterly breaking apart
To come together tenderly. There is love of children.
Should the children become too independent, there is love
Again of the mate. There is love in old age. There is
Love of old age. Love of night, the dew, silence, the northwest.

Night

Whereas last night the full moon made the night resemble a cold day
Today clouds give the night its old shrouded, crowding demeanor.
Ghosts stalk the forest gleaming (at me) from just beyond the circle of
    light thrown by the fire.
You, old night, I wish to make my peace with.
Eventually I know even I (I think, I'm told) must enter naked, a cold north
    wind in winter or a gentle September breeze instructing my sole spirit . . . .

There exist powers overwhelming for the human body and mind.
The aborigine's untold night of meditation on the mountain, coming
    away with his life-long totem and power.
The mountains tonight are alive with benevolence that could (for one
    lacking humility and respect or the hunter's perspicacity) flame up
    into insane malevolence.
You, old complete night, I wish to make my peace with
Being utterly a creature of the water and the light.

Night on the mountain, the human animal alone, without cohorts,
    speech and music inane without other ears to listen
Yet blasting, blasting against the night
Even after fire dies, its skin still the halo beacon to nothing in nothing,
Mind pouring on the electricity, outward to friends back in the cities
Receiving in return only strange sounds.

The ear must differentiate and protect.
Just as fluids within keep the body balanced so must the ear when the
    eyes are blinded by night
Balance the mind. Eyes, heroes of the day, enjoying orgiastically autumnal
    delights
Are now slaves to every primeval passion of the mind.
But the ears: it is a sound they have heard before and can identify.

Night, old strange night (were we once acquainted?), I wish to be at peace
    with you by becoming knowledgeable.
Fear like fire clings to its fuel.
I wish to dampen passionate fears by attuning the five senses to all that is
    normal dark and day.
To know the habits and cycles of everything I live beside
And my inner spirit become a silent tide attuned to nature's lunacy.

Absolutely Smooth Mustard

I prefer to sleep and dream

I prefer to sleep and dream than face
this solitary room. No pity, I go on
without a drink and look with gay eyes on
my future in a forest or a city, someplace.

It's very amusing, what a middle class boy
like me came to, isolated in the northwest
corner of this island, caught in the deepest
loneliness and yet in my heart all this joy.

Surrounded by buildings I am not at peace
yet strangely I am, not like a zen
master but as a man in the wind who when
most despairing and oppressed is most released.

Old records, old unloved books. Sara's cheek
is a source of pleasure, but she has a friend
with whom to share it and can depend
on him for companionship throughout the week.

So I ride the subway home. I look at faces
and they look at mine, mute, animated spirits.
A crazy woman pushes aboard and exhibits
herself. To her, the passengers' glances are caresses.

Not enough heat

Not enough heat. Snow. Cold. and now rain
on Tuesday morning. traffic sloshes to work.
it is cloudy for the second straight day. the snow
was magical only for an hour. businesses might
have closed. now it's melting in a cold rain.

is the city depressing me? i ride the subway
and the people no longer seem beautiful. the noise
is just noise, no longer the power of God. i sit
slumped, still at ease, but no longer playing
with the eyes of other passengers. glance at the ads
and then go to sleep with my eyes open.

it is winter, and it should have its effect. the
difficult, dangerous season when weak creatures die
and the strong barely survive. why expect
much heat to mitigate it and the happiness of Spring?
accept cold and discomfort and the bad sound made.
it is a poor city, the seasons touch us. there is
not enough heat. snow. cold. and now rain.

Almost Spring

Almost Spring but only February
almost February but only January
only January but almost March.

Almost everyday I play my trumpet
almost every night I ride the trains
every midnight I'm on the trains.

Almost every morning I turn on the radio
every weekday I go to work
every midnight I ride the trains home.

Everyday I spend at work
almost every weekend I play the trumpet
Saturday I ride the train downtown.

Almost every night I get some sleep
only everyday I go to work
every midnight I'm on the trains.

Almost Spring but only February
almost February but only January
only January but almost March.

Chinese Sonnets

I

These days I forgive myself everything. After all
I'm alone and unhappy so I give myself a little treat
whenever possible. On summer nights I remember
the good women who loved me but live with their husbands now.

This is not an easy life but I'm not afraid. Despair
leads me to talk too much about myself rather than
be transcendent. I trade push for shove with the world
and sitting above the river feel I could move the globe.

If I could stay out here on the roof all day,
get stoned and read the I Ching, write a few lines
and forget my troubles, I could be happy
today. Then I would go to work tomorrow.

But I rise at dawn and drink some orange juice.
It is good with ice. Buy a newspaper going to the train.

II

In this lousy life we work five days a week.
An Indian could gather a week's food in three days
and go swimming in the hot afternoon. The pleasure
civilization offers is a drive past fast food joints
on Merrick Avenue to a sea food restaurant in Freeport.

Almost everyone I know is dissatisfied with life
as we have been pressed into it. The system gives us
cancer and heart attacks and repressed sexuality when
I was born to be sensuous and enjoy another's body.
Instead I slug the world and the world slugs back.

I have five minutes to finish this poem. I remember
the smooth women I have known, remaining in bed
all morning. Our big ambitions are our curse.
We uphold our end of the society.

III

While it's true that I'm not happy, I'm very amused
at the craziness I have let myself in for.
Hopefully it's only one year of sleeping in my clothes
without a woman and drinking plenty of wine after work.

I listen to someone start a car downstairs, but that
is not my world, nor do I know any of these eight million
I live beside in the crotch of many waters. Above
Broadway Saturday, the geese fly south for winter.

This morning, in twenty minutes, I will go downstairs wearing
a shirt and tie and jacket and carrying a briefcase.
I will tear myself from the pleasures of tea and breakfast
to arrive at the office where each day my happiness is challenged.

I accepted humanity as a natural part of nature. When
I did that I had to pay the rent and get a job, too.

IV

A famous samurai crosses a plain in winter
looking for work. He comes to a farm community
but the farmers have no use for his skills. So
he removes his swordbelt and sets to work digging.

It is temporary employment while the seasons change.
The sky is gray and all of the women are occupied
warming their homes. None look up from their work
except to glance at the strong samurai digging.

Why is he digging in the frozen ground? The poet
knows little about farming and less about fighting.
He has put the samurai to work at a pointless task.
It is too early in the year to begin digging.

Nobody pities the pointless samurai or gives him food.
He ties on his sword and starts chopping wood.

V

These bird songs, this January morning, I look
for a way out of life. The Texas woman tells Marc
stories about the football players she's fucked.

Although I complain like a blue jay about it, life
has accepted me. Walking uptown with Stephanie it's clear
how much the Empire State Building I've become.

Nevertheless, we make our own decisions. To fight war
or not. They are all my friends, I work for their success,
but choose my poison independently. For me, laziness
and anonymity when I could have been a star.

Newspapers indicate there is much to discuss besides myself
but the Muse seems to disagree. My few friends and the age
will look quaint as a daguerreotype in the light
of the holocaust. I kiss the girl of my dreams.

VI

Again it is almost Spring. It gives me only pain
to think back on past Springs when I seem to have been
someone else. The people who lived then live today
in the same bodies but changed in every other way.

Of course I must continue, with or without good humor.
What was amusing in my youth, that God's finger
could move me to another square, now makes me fear
old friends who are dead to me and yet still here.

The veil of life is thin if one doesn't believe in mystery.
Frequently it blows and reveals the thickening body,
alone, without a soul. One hopes for a consort who
through her own pain has become gentle and simple too.

If only I could share this life with a good wife.
But she would only be unhappy and bring me grief.

South Bronx

While I'm reading a poem about it on the previous page
the girls come over to visit their boyfriends and dance
in high shoes and perfume. Their legs are strong and their voices high.
And the guys get high and hard thinking about what the girls are like
    behind their eyes.

That says more about me than reality. And it's exactly four lines.
Ken Patchen would say his angel smells sweet and sassy.
I feel the bony fingers of mine who has been working to stay alive.

Enough small poetry. One must conceive of a project–
say a poem about a bridge–or stop writing
and instead walk over the bridge at sunset and see the city in a nuclear war
the clocks, the Watchtower and the docks gone and no smoke.

I still exist but I'm late for my job. I'm dressed well
in honor of true love and Spring which both outlast the holocaust.
The manager cans me with the cold hard eyes of one who accepts the
    rules entirely.

Goodbye to the rows of dead metal desks and goodbye
to those who can take it longer than I.

The kids downstairs do not read poetry and very little prose.
The General Theory of Employment, Interest and Money does not occupy
    their minds.
The sex pistils of the mountain daisy is no concern of theirs
And the guy upstairs who plays the horn is less than a curiosity but makes
    more noise.

When I feel like this nothing matters and this is good–
get warm with wine, turn out the lights and turn up the radio–
if only there were a woman who liked the down and out life too.

In the end someone sticks a gun in my face in the South Bronx.
How I got among the fire escapes in the sooty alley I cannot say
but it is one of my earliest memories. Perhaps it is my grandmother
    holding my hand
or one of the clowns. I say drop that fucking gun and he blows me away.

For Spring No Hesitation Is Great

Today is April 1st. Transit strike.
Mayor Koch accepting the fact. Myself,
far from crisis central, in North
Manhattan, measuring the temperature
of my apartment. In the sun it is
warm. The crows have returned again
for Spring.

Today life and the city are o.k. Watching
cat in the morning sun. Drinking tea.
My 1300 dollars will melt like summer
snow, but in the meantime, like samurai
I do not show my fear. I remain still
as on the subway and prepared to fight.

I am sitting under the emergency brake
when a coiffured Latin woman rushes aboard.
The doors close but she decides she wants
out. She bangs on the door as the train begins
to move. I see it happen on her face,
she finds the red cord and pulls,
no hesitation.

Maybe someone's hand or foot was caught
in the door. Maybe she's just selfish and
impetuous, got on the uptown not the downtown
side. Maybe the friends she could have
been with didn't get aboard. Whatever
her reason, she acted and the train obeyed.

Some of the passengers sit through the
whole thing, some of us stand. Myself,
I stand, look for the hand caught in the door.
Later, walk home through the pouring rain.
Today is April 1st. Transit strike.
Sky blue, temperatures mild. Democracy
is great.

How cool!

How cool!
this early summer evening
after a day so oppressive
even we New Yorkers move painstakingly.
The breeze in sumac trees
so why am I not more content?
The electricity went off at the bank,
spontaneous bank holiday,
so I'm broke, drinking water.

All my needs except love
fulfilled. Woman
opens her windows. How cool!
this summer evening
in New York, dense New York
the jets overhead
the people on the ground suffering
and struggling toward vague goals
or goals clear as Harry Helmsley's.

How cool and refreshing
this glass of ice water
after today's hot pavement, clothes.
During the afternoon heat
I sleep in my underwear.
What a city I murmur to myself
looking at its map. Big,
Jamaica Bay to Inwood,
the Battery to Pelham Bay.

Nowadays novels need
a few cities to move the plot.
New York, Saigon, Paris.
The protagonist
does not walk in the park. He
uses his car to get around fast.
How cool this evening in New York!
Lost among the bars and industry,
moonrise over Bronx.

Change

I am feeling the shock of fast change. How to cope with it is of course the question. Listen to Beethoven through the neighbor's window? Look up from the page? Appreciate doves even though they are so numerous? I seem to have limitless choices although this cannot be true. Could I have become a computer specialist? Sure! How to remain still in the ever-maddening mandala. To remain still on the outer edge of the wheel is to ride laughingly and pluck at the gold key. I force myself down into the craw of the black vortex New York until I feel the strong oscillations gather rhythm and expel me or accept me.

What do I find within the black electric walls of this unique vortex? I find there is more space between people than I'd ever dared to hope. That my efforts are unnecessary and hopeless. I cancel my subscriptions and stop eating. I embrace wild roots and run through streets with arm around my girl.

★   ★   ★

What is important.
That question.
I part my lips in the middle
   and blow
eat corn chips, dipsy doodles
make love, eat grapes.
                    In their mere chronology
events have no relation. How was making love
different from eating grapes. Differentiation

is essential to bring order from chaos. The chaos
is the accelerated change created by our own species
whose consummations have a quantum effect
   on the environment.
                  But the chaos
existed long before, and long after us
in both more serene and violent forms.
Again a duality, but here's why.
                For
each duality may then be said to be in a dual
relationship with another duality, forming
cubes.

These cubes are difficult to join
with other cubes, unless first they are
somewhat melted.
                    We were traveling among
these cubes, maneuvering
through a static array of equidistant points
but finding it impossible to avoid striking them.

So why the difficulty adapting. Because no species
before us had to adapt to its own effects upon
environment? No, every species must

but our adaptations (of the world) are so successful
(such fabrications!) One green, one brown

                    Two dead leaves
                        sleep-touching
                            Then a breeze!

            ★   ★   ★

                    Loveliness and loneliness
                    these periodic
                    auras
                            they sleep apart/together

    sometimes not always
        using sheets of white nothing madly
            connecting, splicing, parturition
                continuing to birth life and ideals
                    like ants or any other species.
                    Tree, each poem, begins
                        and ends and giving up
                            to life's forms
                                graciously

surrendering to greater force, power, strength
whatever it is called, the clog of heels
upstairs to the door, turning of
the key, the taking out of the
garbage down below, car
starting, placed in
gear, cat
meowing

anyway, for myself, personally, speaking only
for myself, because although the Parks
Department rakes the leaves as it
did last autumn, to keep them
from clogging the sewer system,
I am in a heightened
state of vibration
Quivering

like a long steel pipe banged hard against an
iron beam. The hard hat feels it in
his hand (on the gears) but
great buildings are built that
nature destroys in time
with a little wind
water, fire

air, you glide down through the limpid air
toward the ninety-seven story abandoned structure
remnant of an earlier civilization
abandoned but not yet entirely
swept away in slow waves
of change.

Material Life

Absolute science and art of being whole
            at one and under no delusion that
                        mankind (or nature) give a shit
                                    whether you amount
                                                to something or not.
                                                            Narrowed down
                                                                        nothing

nothing but matter matters, matter, content
            of life (serious, love it) hate
                        death, for the hell of it, to
                                    see what it's like in
                                                the heart of
                                                            darkness.

Deeper and deeper I go
            but who would bother to kill me
                        or love me? Belonging to the drums
                                    of wooful war I
                                                woof and bay like
                                                            every other
                                                                        dog.

Down I go to the depths of material life
            the material is spirit wrought
                        by the material world. The
                                    drum and jet plane
                                                the bird and sumac
                                                            the pollen
                                                                        seed.

No answer is forthcoming for the young fool
            importunes to ask too frequently
                        the fool's question. What
                                    is my next move. He
                                                steps lightly and does
                                                            not seem to care
                                                                        quite where.
                                                                                    The

material world is reality, my friend
and sadness is the spiritual root
without which the love-nut
may be reached only
by stretching
the emotions
bare

raw, where desert delights exhibit
movement in the sunlit light. Where
none find their way
without following leaders
sometimes the wrong way.
The path
is

apart from the dance or the dancer who
cutting cross country laughs
at his perennial fright of being
caught outdoors, out of sight
alone with the wind and rain
for days on end
in hiding.
Up

on the roof, the telephone ringing,
books getting delivered to the library free,
gratis, no fight, no love
a meager understanding
of what rolls
the earth.
Gravity

rolls the earth (and may sometimes rock it)
each of us achieving the gravity of a planet
and pulling the world apart with our loves.
Taking existence beyond the limits

                    set for it, into
                              the universe
                                        beyond

We went out beyond the surf
        into the adirondack of trees waiting,
                wanting nothing, mountains
                        wanting to grow slowly.

This World of Dew

I see a green tree. It is all I want.
A dry rocky mountain and a hawk
satisfy. To die spiritually in
the hot sun and the body go on
climbing. To take the paths among
the rocks and mahogany bush.
To feed on rock lichen and blue
sky. To not need a house.

To leave my mind in the foothills.
To climb everything but blind. In
the deer shade of the cool aspens.
Forgotten by the work force and the shrew.
Bored as a badger disturbed at
its stream. Free singing as the stream
cutting the gorge. Cool as a hummingbird
in its wet spray. Caterpillar fur.

I stay in the mountains unknown.
The roof soot of the city calls me back.
The museum women shaking their bodies
at the stuffed tigers. The meditating
curators and entrepreneurs. Burro.

★   ★   ★

Old Basho, early Spring, took fond leave of his friends,
closed his small house at edge of village,
and with one peasant companion climbed the long narrow road to the North.

Blessed morning!
    the day I left life behind
        but not this world of dew.

Peaches

Wherever peaches grow I go and pick 'em.
When they get ripe I try and swipe 'em.
The farmer runs out with a shotgun and wonders where's the varmint gone?
I'm hiding by the railroad tracks stacking the peaches I've found.

Then a freight train about a mile long rolls by hauling a bucket of rain.
I hop aboard while beautiful clouds gather to the north.
I put my peaches in the bucket and lug it to a hidden part of the train.
The rain begins, the night looms in, it's summer and it's thoughts and warm.

To the clacking rumble and the patter I close my eyes and dream.
An earthquake swallows up the people who wear horrible masks of fright
    as their daily tasks are trampled.
In a favorite movie theater an illumined lady puts her hand in mine,
    warm mouths, breath, skin, hair wing-soft, whole bodies, wind, bare.
I open my eyes at sunrise there's a steady glow of light around.

If you can believe in God, you can believe the mountains go from purple to
    green.
While the last partier meanders home to bed the first farmer is up to milk
    his bread.
Fruit of the world ripens audibly and cities make a silent, distant sound.
Kind of a lonely guy stretches, rubs his eyes, pees out a passing train, has
    a breakfast of peaches and rainwater.

To Eat a Continent Is Not So Strange

1

Waves could wash away certain blue memories but they're too blue. Today I've sat in two places, my heart full of you and how in the night under a half man in the moon too soon, too soon, did love die? Today I've sat in two watery places but the rhythms will never wash away the face and smell and voice of you. Thus, I stand in the sun, like that, the breeze gently tears my beard and life becomes death.

No, no, not that. A boat being repaired in a boatyard. And think of it! people on the planet earth! And nothing, but nothing, not even tao, is permanent. Whereas for us my dear this is a disadvantage, since I wished to be permanently a member of your arms, for me the individual I do not disappear as long as there is change. Life is like all things that are forever changing but will always remain the same. Love is one of those things.

From hitch-hiking, as the sun descends I proclaim this, the mystery more powerful than the handshake. Thus, even unto children I have kept my silence, and even unto you I will. The white birch bending over the river fell in. It carried downstream and in one tidal sweep became a great white fish. When the sea dried up this unlucky fish grew wings anyway and became the great bird. The heavens were too small and it shattered into bits like you and I. A fable.

To say I love you until the house falls down. Beyond the row of houses lit by street lamps and into the night I go, with and without you, both. How is it the powerful night attends you like a magician his queen? The way the sun would climb into a bottle to please me.

2

Under a full night of black night stars, shooting and shining, turning a world of sun worlds, everything universe and cool wind, mountains of dark sound and a stream's breath song, I think often, until dawn, of your strong love. All of these true things becoming mine as a shore. And we inside as a breath baby. Listen, life darling long, four horses grazed nearby my head last night, like good luck. Struck thus I write: your love is greater than the real celestial globe.

Something thicker and velvet than deep sea foam for you swirl lover. Something true to the events of our lives, the clear mountainous horizon of vision. Over the vast green earth O population of human and animal lovers to chewing very cud, our bond is fulfilled as a mother. A tremendous earthquake couldn't exist without us.

Searching for Symbols in a Town Without a River

I begin the day buying yogurt in a small
favorite grocery store. The clerk
a man of few pretenses was making jokes
about his wife, how they fight in bed.
Discovering the better stores in the community.
In a given day, isolated from friends,
I speak to few people. An old woman
asks me for directions to the post office
or I speak to a stranger over the phone about night work.

At home my every thought comes to the counterpoint of a dream:
a girl I love surprises me by knocking on the window.
I ply my arts all day alone.
After this silence like being hidden away in the woods
in a cabin, bored
but owing no member of society an explanation,
invitation to a party. A flow of wine and devilish drugs
and quickly I am making a fool of myself.

My new friends like me
but when they think about me at all,
they wonder.
                    Wandering home
through the midnight air, alone again,
free, admiring
the ghostly houses of my new neighbors
by new moonlight.

Penetrating the Unknown

While waiting but not watching for the sun to set, perhaps the bullfrogs are creating the shadows with their croaks, my friend screams out because he has been bitten by a fly. He is not quiet enough so the flies obtain special pleasure from teasing him. Meanwhile bluebirds skirt the lake surface like the most perfectly designed fighter planes in twos or threes and argue rising up on their tails into the air. While insects prey upon and tease the bare flesh and blood of we humans, they fear the silent violence, the sudden huge presences of these family birds.

A larva with a leaf tip for a cocoon descends a white birch by a long thread. We free ourselves from our writings to observe phenomenon. Then thinking about dinner. The flight of J. Krishnamurti, the eagle guru says even artists (after physicists and mathematicians) may penetrate the unknown if not too absorbed in their own emotions and imaginations. We common people too who loving our wives can love everyone.

What eyesight the bluebirds have to swoop the lake from shore for a flying insect or descend from fifty feet on a thin straw grass and return to chew absent-mindedly! Just fun having song sung among men. As for the syntax, a daisy could swing it unthinking and coast. Along the beehive rocks ants crawl on connecting interlacing instructions. All around us and inside too as if stars were unseen but present it's true. So a man desires breakfast with his lady; could it be more amusing, material or smell?

As the eyesun descends below spun clouds, spirit or the eagle or the drum? Round. The dialectic obscure couldn't be more better said. So round and serious. To love everyone with clearer vision than a bluebird or a lake is to transcend the innocence of insect and take flight action and feed the babies of fate. Phew! Dinner outside the cocoon. I brought myself a student upon the hill or mountain and said to myself I said Obo rebop in summer sweater and what less overweight can carry test uphill so slow? Presently, reformed, informed by the bluebird's eagle spirit, clear cleanhead, I return coagulating mightily ideas the bites of insects ow! to breakfast home and everywhere unknown. Hearing bird with clear conscience echo make.

Morning Chores

As if the sun intended this habitual tendency to make the body healthy I do. First, the brain believes itself what a mistake if it's blue. The eyes blue breeze sky praise God some beautiful living world earth. Good as a proper prayer could good. Then a leg moves. What a miracle course of muscle goes to greatness human and divine. Morning moving as good a feeling.

An arrow of cloud on the sky points the way. Everyday look you and you find an ancient new way. A list of the components contains the river's horizontal reserve deep dull and dark as a dream, the blue sky and her daughter the gentle breeze and her great husband the morning sun. After these, men and their nice machines and their morning chores.

When I get up I brush my teeth mundane. I put fruit in a bowl by the bed and brew tea. I feed the cats animal meats preserved and cans of caught fish organs and oils complex. Their shits being different from mine cleaning. I sweep the floors with a broom and a dust. And knock in the nails. I check the mailbox and search the street a fence a neck a stretch for the mailman and imagine the mail. My doing this opens the windows and unlocks the doors.

Next I water thirty thirsty plants important. The ferns smell of earth spray. This good thing lasts into the wee hours of your life remember. Open goodness goes to heaven sky on earth or in a sense four seasons. I open the back door porch and a black cat morning. You wonder why. A childhood breeze makes the feelings in the mind play music. The mystery of night is now a mystery of morning. Something of nostalgia wine.

The center the stomach the body the sex. It propels the people's body all day. From morning to night a woman a man. Everything fitting and grand and in through the door healthy, nothing and wise. The grass on the hill of a willing riverbank. Welcome and good morning.

Rain

Five days of steady rain. A hurricane approaches the city. The streets are flooding but the wildlife is thriving. Every person wears a raincoat or carries an umbrella. Indoors is cozy. Movie theaters are crowded in the early afternoon. We who live alone are more isolated; those who live together are more aggravated. The heavens are having a fine time belting it out.

A fly is swept from a windowpane in early August but men's machines are almost oblivious to the storm. Except the wires in Mr. Glyckman's Volvo are wet. People's dreams begin to take place in the water. When they awake their thoughts are floating in the puddle of night.

Raindrops slap the leaves and splash the ground. Travel is not advised, wherever you are it seems like home. Next month dirt on the shingles of the house will remind the painter of the great rain. Even the rain no longer makes an impression on the earth, only a ripple in the rain. If there are mountains or the sea they seem more like brother and sister than father and mother these days. Summer feels like winter.

Children are less visible and mothers are women who were once girls. Nightclubs are full and the listeners listen more seriously. Music continues but the rain muse has her say. Lovers are less joyous and more happy. The full moon's influence is muted by clouds, the blood between people is thicker. The Himalayas come to the Rockies and the Rockies reach for the Alps. The imagination comes to the market.

The roads leading down to the river are empty and wet and the bright painted houses along them are quiet. A dog and a cat under a porch patient and unperturbed. A love-gnarled man with a brown beard and walking stick walks in the middle of the street. If a curtain moves, a woman wonders how many days he's been out in the rain like a child. But only the water winding back to the sea, a mad naked saint at the Last Judgment, welcomes him home.

Open Air Market, Ottawa

A sky west crowded domain Ottawa and agreeable future. So says the peace of mind in accordance with the finger weather. By a beer bar beet-faced friendly working men and women chattering about like a lonely conversation. Numerous searches for a friend simple. A street clean courtesy of fruits and legumes grown by the pickers and sold by their daughters speak french on the corner. Blessed by love of success, good money and people, her black hair begets wind, red kerchief and enthusiastic cackle. Through tea window, patchwork colours of canvas fruit stalls, ducks and hens caged, carrots, peppers and radishes, fifty acres of garden farm soil. Delicious Ontario farmland. Given the highway, given the tall building, given the helicopter scan for presence, in their orderly height of confusion. Welcome the berries to the sumac bush.

It's the great nonsense leaf I believe in. The rum skunk, the back grove. One cloudy day is bigger than the whole war television to me. That's how I watch a girl selling vegetables so enthusiastically she doesn't see me. One ambrosial diversion is permissible: the invisible language music love. Generations of children kingdom come. Whatever your pleasure myself and my friends have tasted of your concerns. One by one we cross the continents making big mistakes. The all-knowing farmer God as you know him patiently understands us but doesn't give a damn. It is this freedom that makes me laugh. I walk the crowded streets of every city and every soul is a naked strip tease of ecstatic light. Nothing could be dirtier than these amorous open books to me. They so excite me that I must consult my wisdom for guidance.

When a girl on a bicycle smiles, that is a smile. You have examined a leaf, a rock and a brain and you have painted a sunset with your human ways. My circles of boat thought drift wider and wider into a concentric nothing. You are so detailed and great and I am nothing as air. I blow you away and together we float in a parade of delight.

White Waits

Rather than put myself in the sky which is so
complete with blue and clouds, I make a space
in a line of people climbing a trail in the mountains.

All night I work on my thinking and waiting
until at dawn I see the iron clouds shift sunlight
and listen to the years changing my life with a laugh.

I say thank you to all the influences that a plant
like me goes on growing fearless as a daisy.
I need no robes, I wear baggy underpants in the morning.

By afternoon I am transformed by the light from my beard.
Some girls think I'm cute. At first I'm shy but soon
I take my wooden chair among a bench of kids from Waltham.

At night I fall in love with the first person to stop
his car. Because I am a well of love for my lady.
The drone of stars slowly changing places in the sky.

When I fall asleep by the river it is like I'm dead.
There it is. I use my coat for a pillow and lay my head
at the root of a tree. Shade my eyes from the sun, white waits.

In a Day

The one power that a man can have is in
the perfection of himself. He changes
with the weather but of this he's unaware.

A churlish man and his teacher are walking
along a road when he is suddenly instructed
to look down a side street. Spring trees in leaf.

I go in front of the mirror and observe
the changes to come in my face. I turn
my chair so I can see out all the windows.

What is right fits the time perfectly. It
is all out of my hands. In this the peace
is supreme. Yet my hands embrace the pot.

In the morning the air is cold and clear
at the river. Then clouds and the confusion
in people. At dusk the sky is clear again.

The Canopy of Stars

Women are not inspired to love me. This
must be an oversight on the creator's part.
Even in my beard I'm built handsomely as other men.
The women vaguely discern a weakness in my character.
About the loins? They scent it out. I dine alone.

As a communal artist this is so, also. The other
musicians choose the saxophone. I am, of course,
unconcerned and in no hurry. In my own time
I will come into my own. In the meantime
I have the canopy of stars it seems to myself.

I take a walk beneath them through the neighborhood.
They are soothing in the way people are not. Both
give joy, of course, but people burn me up while the stars
cool me down. Very cool beneath the canopy of stars.

Absolutely Smooth Mustard

There is absolutely nothing to do. Some people
fall in love. I go have a cheese sandwich
with mustard. Watch skyscraper lights from
the bed. Look at the books and decide to read
none of the dry words. The cheese sandwich is
good, and orange juice. It's cold in the kitchen
so I go back to bed even though it's Spring.

Some people go dancing in fish net stockings.
They find a good time—but exactly what this means—
it's not more important than a star. Quite
what is this waiting. Tonight I could disappear
and the world might not miss me until next year.
I remember passionate nights with some of the women
I've known. Two sides of a smooth stone.

The Dark Green Conifers

another day in the woods. on Strawberry ridge
looking out over undulating green hills to
the next great wall ridge of mountains. the last
morning clouds left from last night's storm
hanging in the valley mistily. the sun eventually
burns them away.

the respect between old Paul Karlsen and I continues
to exist. even though he's a Mormon and I'm a fallen
New Yorker. the work is comparatively easy, lifting
hundred pound bags, so you can just imagine what
we do other days. in fact, it's fun, especially for
young Bates. we get all white (and our lungs dusty).

on the way to and from the work site I read
in Silent Spring, the chapter against herbicides, gathering
inspiration for the upcoming controversy. in the end
perhaps I'll be fired for refusing to lay down Tordon
beads. realizing this, as I drive with Bates,
I see the dark green conifers and begin to miss them.

Rocks and rattlesnakes, bluebells
and mountain daisies, grasses and cactuses, mahogany
bush, lodgepole pine and quaking aspen, lush forest
and dry sun-tortured mountainside, wind and seed
carried by wind, ants, streams, hummingbird
and hawk, deer, badger, ground squirrel, wolverine.

Snake Creek

Tired body aches. Long walk on starry night–
ears attuned for bear at creek, or cougar.
Nothing, not a doe.
                    But that afternoon
came upon a healthy young buck in a meadow.
High up. And a hawk left a feather for me.
Old, old stands of lodgepole pine, grey bark
like wrinkled hides of elephants. Thick carpet
of dead needles.
                    Thirst. Sit at snowbank
for an hour eating snow. Burn tongue.
To soon after stumble upon a pond and the place
that a creek springs from the mountain. Water
indescribable. Eat ravenously and drink deep
gulps.

Climb highest rocky peak at dusk. Razor-back
ridge. Mother hawk scream nearby. Must
backtrack and then go straight down near dark
feet fall through layers of scrub pine, hands
grab for the live stalks only support against
broken bone.
                    Choose steep narrow bed of loose rocks,
surely waterfall in some other season and descend
on ass and all fours, feet first always fearful that
it will end in an uncontrollable hundred foot drop.
Trickles of water nearing bottom.
                              Cracked hands, raw
behind, cross final snowbank and attain road
along Snake Creek.

Brother Death

Take the Ripe Plum

How far from nature and life it is

the gray clouds, airplanes in them

the night cooing and pigeons roosting

Sirma's garden gone to roses and seed

        That airplane overhead!

        pointing the way

        pointing to war

War being an aggravated condition of what
we already know

        Flowering beneath the noise

of yet another jet passing overhead.

        ★   ★   ★

Why this much sadness in a world so beautiful?
We are sad for the weariness of everything, including earth
(that will go on tropically flowering long after we are gone)
we

        who are nothing
        in powerful time's
        grip

history, passionate history, coffee between
neighbors.

        ★   ★   ★

        Enter into alliance
        With the sweet darkness, night!

Night and day, day and night
Everybody knows when the moon is bright.

We dance by the light of the moon
All night.

★   ★   ★

We dance by the light of the moon.
We dance by the light of the moon and setting sun.

                    We drive
            we crow and call
three pigeons!
            and make the world alive
                    even bricks.

                    Jets
two pigeons!
            Milk-skinned doves
                    enmesh

                    Two gray-skinned sharks, jets,
embrace in the sky, a blue green oil truck takes
the hill, cobblestoned, in low
steady gear.

★   ★   ★

Zazen position
    to remain so
        unmoved
            yet moved
                by the stillness

the movement of the car uphill
    part of your system of beliefs
        unmoved by it, parked

necking in the front seat
                hawks diving for pigeons' eggs

and so you are compelled to move
        by the force that created you. but
                you impose your own small order
                        departing from traditions
                                human history understands

        a mutant

such as those currently developing
the human mind beyond its past capacities.

         ★   ★   ★

                Two straw sandals
                        blue jay call
                                two sea gulls

         ★   ★   ★

The jets return
        flying low.
                Laying low

and breathing low
        mists
                of pure noise.

Monk's shaved pate

Monk's shaved pate
thick pelt around edge
leans over book

        leans over book above river
reciting lines, reading scriptures, preparing
first for his personal salvation, then
for those of other men.

        He prays, sweetly
        serenely, steadfastly
        participating

in the broad rhythmic thrusting of the river
and the earth.

        Completely exposed
      to its vibration
    he vibrates passively
yet passionately

putting effort into remembering some
    of the ancient, past taboos
      and practices
        Performing

the art of total presence
and abstinence.

        Absent from worldly
          life, abstaining wholly
            from touching
              the black girl

        becoming
       part of her beads
     her sweaty underwear

commanding a full dress view
    of her stimulus,
      her honey.

Bone Music

1

Last night dinner
    with four other couples
        and a drunken single girl

points out the difficulties in living together
and apart. One woman, just married,
is clearly a lesbian.

        Even the
son of a wealthy doctor, disdainful of
inebriates more artificial than the moon,
full, full of joy for humanity
and life
        suffers deepening depressions
like the dark outside a lamplight.

It was a good restaurant
expensive but comfortable
in the alternate life-style way
the cook was a hairy
talented clown
and we clowned though beneath each
facade
was turmoil and decay.
        We lay
beside each other like bones
in a boneyard
and find joy (I do anyway)
in the bone dance
to bone music.
        How I love bone music!
the freedom within communality
comrades in our individual weaknesses
but powerful with the totemic voice.

        This turmoil
        this music
        I cannot make order of it
        I care not to

2

Without a thought for slash fuel
or deer, the mist
deepens and deteriorates upon
the mountain. The mountain
completely unaware
of its greenness. The ice
is centuries old.

A red-tailed hawk
floats above the unit
observes what small mammals, birds
are in the clear-cut

Awaits
the moment
to strike

or fades away almost
silent as the mist. I dream
of it, though I am awake
among my co-workers, the bullet
system zinging cut logs down
to the road, firewood.

3

Pardon
me you mountains
for coming to the edge
without mystical knowledge
or belief, only love and wrinkled
eyes for the women and men who
light the fires and wield the chain saws,
drive the cat, swing the ax, I

completely laugh among them like a god
yes, although my face is a mask of hate
and pain, what god does not come to this field

of flowers out of fear and confusion and chains
product of the hot anvil and hot engine
of human history

> Remember, poet
> cold indifference
> Arctic ice

this duality, these arm-breaking dualities
this volcanic eruption erupting from some
confluence of beheaded forces, one
powerful with eternity, one
blinding with intensity, meet
and in the middle is me.

You mountains, you dinners
tear me apart with the pleasures of living
like a husband and wife fighting
like two dogs fighting but not biting
hard, like my old poems (a pleasurable
conceit), life (something serious?)

bests my best synthesis of it, and
I begin to pray, hard to believe
I begin to pray in my poems, I
smile but I begin to pray, for
this prayer gives no hope, no belief,
no past. I begin to pray

and say nothing but the same words
repeatedly I begin to pray, amazed
for the red brick houses, for the dinner couples
for a happy combination of sun and mist
I begin to pray for nothing I begin to pray
for long life in the lean years I begin
to pray for none of these things
instead I pray without words,
I begin to pray without words.

The World Has Come to Lake Waubeka

New York City summer, summer everywhere, mountains of my past;
picking through the personals for a new girlfriend and finding sixteen women
     looking for companionship, someone to care about;
basketball with brother of one of my ex-wives;
how it is, as the years pass, birds and motorized vehicles among the constants.

This joy, this sadness, of staying late until eight o'clock at work on Friday night
and then bottle of beer while walking up Ninth Avenue, sunset reflected off
     midtown towers, girl-watching female heroin addicts,
Latino women with cigarette burns on their arms and still I desire their herpes,
     I do not think about the women I loved;
home with nothing to do but read Raymond Chandler or watch Humphrey
     Bogart, go to sleep.

This is life and not life. In thirty years or so I'll be gone from the earth,
     bones whitening on some mountain
or rotting in the lowlands earth, wet, river or estuary I lived near, flesh to
     sweat flesh with the population,
dead. This death consciousness of which should give this life's activities
     perspective, except for the red sunset which remains untouched by
     atomic IQ;
and dead, laying open to the blue sky and dry leaves one autumn like last
     autumn, or the autumn I realized my insignificance

Sunset

Sunset, quiet, except
for happy birthday to neighbor's child,
virgo, and all that means, purity
of morality, inability to scheme,
whatever else the stars dictated.

Woodpecker climbs oak, Connecticut.
Not ten years ago this mountain was
completely forested, untouched
since early arrival of Europeans.
Now my parents' home and others stand
in new clearings. The birds
do not seem to mind. Sing,
and deer occasionally visit, from where?
Out of the pre-historic past.

That I must die
is my every third thought.
On my hands and knees, cold sweat,
my own body murdering me.
I meet death with the philosophy
I lived in life. Acceptance
of the loneliness, the unregarding
beauty. There is that shoreline
along the straits to Puget Sound,
in mist, the generations
of sea birds nesting on the water.

Polar Bear Mugs Wino

Have I ever been profoundly lost? Yes. Railroad tracks and a river wide as the Amazon, yet lost. Living in the intense sunshine of northern New York summer, but lost in the shade of a gazebo. And here? Here I am enclosed in a tomb of porcelain machinery. With another winter passing its calling card in at the window. The warm steam no longer cutting the rough edge. Wearing wool sweater nights. The freedom of summer gone and only one fuck. What a nightmare, what a strange dream, life on planet, winter all around.

A system, they call it a system. I call it an evolved anarchy. Repetition, never. What do I know. Repetition, every two thousand years. Coming of a frost, coming of a fire. When nature proves furious beyond remembrance. Polar bear mugs wino.

★   ★   ★

CUNNILINGUS

Tall, attractive, talented WM, 31,
trumpet player, takes pleasure in
performing cunnilingus with clean
attractive women. Age, race, marital
status no object. All replies answered.

Here is where it started, amusing myself in an undisciplined manner in the playpen. Being rude when interrupted. Height of bad taste hitting the wall, what's he talking about. Marlowe went to bed. He had a headache. Used an empty bottle for a teddy bear/sap. In the middle of the night, three secret men approached the rock he slept under. They did not see him there, the fire had long ago gone out. But they'd seen it across the valley, and tried to estimate. They were close.

What do I care. They did this, he did that, they did this and this and that. He used his feet, took off his shoes. It mauled him to death in two minutes of the first round. Would have been better for him if it happened faster. Never got his knife out of his pocket. But he lived, with one eye after that.

What do you do with a drunken sailor early
    in the morning?
You pull that sailor out of bed by his hairy
    moorings.

Why should anybody believe this, this tiresome outpouring of old moans and groans, grumbles about loneliness of life and dominance of telephone. This gamble on print, above the spoken, sung word. The meditative call to inhabitants of planet to kneel woefully and pray. No, to chant as if the planet were mending.

Mending rhymes with ending, why not. And television, radio appreciated. Drugs and booze, jagged bent faces, black wet rock. The mantle of moss ripped away. Period. Amen to men. Absolute magical ripcord.

Alive

What is appropriate to say about the changes
in your life. That at 23 I was confused
under the sculpted pines about a girl.

Quietly my friends and I contemplate death.
A subject, until recently, unknown
to us in such a variety of forms. Nuclear flash
to exploding blood vessel in the brain, control
eludes us. Heirs to a society adept with numbers,
we run in the park and eat whole grains,
increasing survival odds.

The city and the mountain are two hard anvils
against which our hot lives are shaped. Love
is the fire, and the need for love. To be shaped
by the lover's warm hands, like clay.
Alive, almost sure of it.

No cows to look at

No cows to look at
I hear the truck traffic

Everything changes like clouds
The page this poem is on burns

Coming from the funeral with friends
Talking on the telephone

No trucks to grind their gears
I hear the minute hand moving

Birds and people inhabit the earth
A black bear inhabits the earth, too

A rock in the sun
Calligraphy brush

In a mind there is apocalypse
No one can hear it

Crows, bluejays and pigeons

Crows, bluejays and pigeons
talk this morning. Closest we come
to wilderness here. Autos screech
and sirens scream. Only 7 a.m.
My fat belly and possible cancer
worry me. With a few months
to live, I'd search the wilderness
for some wisdom I missed. Or
plain beauty of natural randomness.
Knowing that, why do I remain
in health? I must devote my
present to my future existence.

The bluejays complain long after
everyone else is silent.
Love and friendship need the body
and society. You belong, you want
to belong, three days in wilderness
and you gladly return to
lovers' arms and plumbing.
But one day you die. And this
is the ideal independence you sought.
This death is the pristine aloneness,
the untouched wilderness and
freedom from necessity! And
it is certain. You do not save
for it. You do not worry that
you may miss your opportunity.

East Harlem to the Grand Tetons

No words, oily body sweats, city summer.
Desperate to get out and never return although
stalled on Triborough Bridge I admired the skyline.

My city, my death, I did it my way.
Counting your blessings a healthy activity,
the park out my back window, a job that pays.

But I am losing strength to fight
for the world in my imagination. Acceptance of reality
makes me a fossil of society.

Basho in old age found strength to walk
deep into the mountains. He visited famous sites
up north. Po Chu-i traveled mountains in his dreams.

You can leave at any time. You can return
without being seen. A way to learn
your insignificance, freedom to have never been.

Jet, cracked paint, tea

The clouds take a little blue from the sky
beyond, how beautiful the weather makes life
seem. The sky is where the soul goes when
the mind runs out of destinations. We love
the mountains because that's where the earth
meets the sky. If you just watch the sky
an hour each day, lie back in the grass,
you'll never be ill. When it rains your face
becomes a holy bowl. Once I was a beggar, no
cares, by railroad tracks. They too disappeared
into the sky. A small town you could hold in your fist
on the prairie. A big city easy to hold in your mind
when you're in the sky. The clouds take a little blue
from the sky. The sky takes a little blue from your soul . . .

Let us accept this pain

Let us accept this pain
and some fear
it will heighten autumn colours
crack of clean air
black crows in blue sky
lake.

Rather than fight pain, falling
asleep in front of tv,
understand the full
import of its situation
in the body. Blessed
once, cursed now
only fear prevents
full knowledge of experience.

The gray sky brings
winter, no blame.
The poet writes a few last poems
or continues to live with his pain.
In itself pain does not oppose
life, and may enhance it
or build character, create
wisdom. But too much fear
chokes the throat and burns
the eyes. It
destroys the last free
assessment of life.

        ★   ★   ★

Now I am going to live in my body
as it is, almost fearlessly
running in pain, working
to abandon immortality
as a hope, conceiving
sunset after sunset
feeling what I feel.

On the streets I meet
many beautiful young women
curious to a certain extent
what makes a man older.
I can only say ten years
and the hand that reaches through
the cloud. I can say
only the knowledge of mortality
which makes us brothers and sisters
with the animals. And only
the acceptance which gives us wisdom
to couple often and lovingly.

How am I going to live every day
as my last, hoping happiness
outgrows fear by an ounce
or enough? By running, writing
and loving. By moving uphill
and downhill like a bear.
By committing my last words
to a powerful lord. How
do the clouds accept my dead
self? A rock thrown, a crow.

        ★   ★   ★

When I am old
young girls will not be frightened anymore.
I will invite them
to my seat and tell
about the women I knew.
I will tell about
the clothes they wore
and how they earned a living.
I will try to remember
what was important to them
and if they had a favorite color
or knew how to divine.

Maybe I live and maybe I don't.
The smoke is white or black.
The winds are bright or dark.
The coins are heads or tails.
What have I been afraid of?
Death is most of all like sleep.
We spend so long apart
after briefly knowing ourselves.
I need you to know myself
and without you all I know
is sun.

Friends or Mountains

Cold middle of night, fast heartbeat, friends
Christmas
I am close to becoming part poet again
If I live
Words coming from far beyond my mind
Stars
Mountain rocks where blue sheep toe tip tops
Or jazz
The bass line reminding me of love's hurt beat.

It will be a long night, but I can sleep late
Dream
Of work, or what I do together naked with
A woman
I have known. Sandstone mesas west of
Everywhere
Where the wind gives everything the shape of
Old bones
And your wounds heal from their insignificance.

We go on until we die, and we all someday
Die
Joining endless mindless space, and contributing our
Bodies
To pine-cloaked earth where if I had a
Memory
I'd remember edge of forest fires I had fought
And warm
My ghostly hands against the thought. But
No
Thoughts or memories remain except in minds of
Friends
And lovers who survive to lift their faces to
The rain.

Is it stress

Is it stress,
or loss, despair and survival
we must discuss.
                    Stress is just the symptom
of a universe intent to destroy the individual
before it births new life. It sends the dogs
after us, after the holocaust, in the tattered ruins
of our city.
                    There is this despair and expectation
of destruction, but somewhere there is still also
simple sky blue,
flowers among railroad ties,
true love between sexual partners.

Is it sex,
or love, companionship and reliableness
we must expect.
                    Sex, nothing but laying my head
at your cunt, can interest me sometimes. Your legs
lead to a pleasure that seems infinite and smells
perfect.
                    So there is this tenderness, a connection
like a suction to the biological that is ephemeral
as snow on the ground,
one elk in aspen,
death and nothing less.

The Shootist

In "The Shootist", J.B. Books is not feeling up to snuff.
He has cancer. What are the concerns
of a man dying.

To die
commensurate with the way he lived his life.
Books dies in a gunfight.
McIntosh dies in the desert, under a broken wagon,
fighting Indians.
Norman Thayer will die of heart failure
by the side of his wife, Ethel.

Two police officers
die investigating a stolen moped at a gas station
in the Bronx.
One buys it between the eyes, the other in the back.
The killer out on early parole
from a manslaughter rap.
The DA blames the judge, the judge blames the parole board,
and the board says the jails are overcrowded.

What should I be doing, old turtle.
Devote myself to re-order the world
or crawl off to a lonely spot and preserve myself.
We are trying
to educate everyone to their individual capacities
and see that all are fed, clothed and sheltered adequately.
Because the suffering of one citizen makes suffering
for another, the slow death of one sometimes makes
the sudden murder of another.

There is this
black rock we live on and its lovely mantle of green.
It is all that is perfect. And everything of it is
perfect that respects its integrity. On the subway
I was amused to find, hidden in the confused
mass of anonymous, bleak graffiti, unseen

by the studied, expressionless passengers,
in pink, delicate script, vertically written,
the word penis.

People are the element I live in.
The world is pushy, we are bone,
the numbers of us overwhelm.
It is going to be hot again soon
and the Bronx will actively resent it.

Books dies in Carson City,
only two or three people will miss him at all.
He died alone as he lived,
with his enemies.

Brother Death

Even in the last days you need clean clothes;
therefore you may be found in the laundry
mornings, small task against the larger one
of not breathing. With simple joy
men may forget to fear their deaths.
Six inches of snow reminds us of its dominance
in a pleasant way. Coming and going of sleep,
circling of the moon around the earth, earth
around the sun. The great man dies
and this makes death more noble for us all.
It is with joy that I accept the pains
that herald my end. I do my job well.
I go to the well and break the ice for water.
The bucket comes up full of dying wonder.

To Have Loved Mary

Today is Sunday and I'm going to the ocean
or maybe not. Definitely not doing the laundry
or maybe I will. Moss and even a small tree
grow in the rotten stubs of the pier pilings.
The city is Seattle and it has a macho airport.

Give me the comfort of a moose knowing its
water supply. The mosquito's acceptance of its position
among a million mosquitoes. The pool of stagnant
water that remains one with the mothering ocean.
I drift on the air, less than a seed, a bacteria.

Or I am human, big dick, big brain containing
universal philosophic affidavit. Pleased by
the churning of my tongue, sexual enlightenment,
devout prayer, gourmet dining. I swear
it is best to be alive and to have loved Mary.

Colonel Bob

No jets but a rooster mornings,
cows and goats. Corn, timber.
What is the relation of New York City
to this. At home on Seaman Ave.,
jets, automobiles, sirens,
glass breaking, pigeons cooing, people going
to work, subways roaring.
We are gathered into cities to make room
for black bears and timber growing.

From the profuse plant life into the swarm
of varicolored people playing basketball
and inhabiting hard buildings. Our social service system
delivers meals and finds jobs. Our dirty streets
support the high heels of our sexual young women.
Produce from the countryside transported
by rail and interstate to Korean immigrants' markets.
After midtown offices empty, downtown nightclubs fill.

It is fun, it is alone in space, it is funny
that we feel we must explode it.
The hairy monkey, man, desires the smooth one,
woman, badly. She is looking nicely at him
through the amber scotch in a subway ad.
Smell urine around somewhere. This is home
and I work to make it happy. The strange women
unafraid. The future satisfying and long lasting.
The world clean and friendly. With my ten thousand
heartbeats, lovebeats, wingbeats.

Chambermaid With Ravens

The Aberdeen bus arrives, deposits and boards
the same people daily. One is the dark-haired
chambermaid at the tourist lodge, awkward
in her print dress and wearing a scowl. Her
breasts look soft although her legs are
not perfect.
         The sun dominates the weather
this summer and with blackened face I buy a
popsicle each day and come closest to distant
childhood. This is what the chambermaid notices
and scowls about–the popsicle and sneakers of
a grown man. On a summer night what passions
would I find in her?
         We take our place in the pattern
of daily activity, pick-up trucks with crews
arriving and leaving, uniformed rangers narrow
in their imaginations. Two ravens fly together
over the unit, the ravens are behaving like hawks
lately, beautifully. Both my memory and sense
of mystery are bowing to knowledge of death.
         Human
society. It takes me along. Our role is not
to understand it all. The wheel on this piece
of machinery, turning of the night around the stars.
Spires of green fir against the sky's blue blue.
If man, the monkey, explodes his earth, will my
bones then float among the stars?
         Children
and the blue green earth are what the chambermaid
and I may share. She and I or another man,
me and the naked women of the past. What weather
there has been this summer, best since '79. Felling
trees in the forest, I look uphill. Two ravens float
like hawks, wind, no sound.

Under-sky sleeping, bone keeping

In the holy spot
with the sitting rock
there is oak. Out
where humans live
there is shagbark hickory
and maple.

Ants climb the rock.
August, and young birds
are quiet when the parents
celebrate the flowering
weeds. Next come
the seeds of autumn.

I am here to name it
and know it and help it
to grow. True, these mountains
are my grave. A good grave
to go to.

The crows have been
in conference, again.
A jay, blue, pokes
a hole through reality.
There I find the sumacs
fruiting and the male sex organs
of the Queen Anne's lace.

Company of flies, so
intelligent. Two abandoned
farmer's fields are wide as
Alaska. Is there one
who could name
every flower here?

Plate Tectonics Versus Gamma Ray Bursters

An old man remembers what he has been
yet the details are unimportant. Then
the outline disappears, and the meaning.

Good, I can die or go to work, be wise
or a jerk. Rich or poor, the wind and rain
wear us away and it's o.k.

Ask what matters, that
question. Feeling the seasons, wearing a hat,
loving your woman, a good shit.

Children born. Two cells meet, multiply,
spiral into fetus. The mother is amazed:
an intelligence apart from herself.

The violent rainstorm kept me awake
although the lightning was still far away.
I lay in my bed and listened naked.

Under Mummy Mountain

Aspen, ponderosa pine, blue spruce
pink glacier-cut rock, scree, ravens
gray jay, peregrine falcon, hawk.

We climb to 11,000 feet in three days,
camp at Lawn Lake for three days. Alpine
tundra. Elk, bighorn sheep, marmot.

Tileston Meadows, ticks in grass,
rock face of Mummy Mountain.
Binoculars show pink cracks in gray rock.

Stoke gas stoves, play cards.
Boil water, set up tarps, lay out
sleeping bags, hang bear bag.

Watch crescent moon slice into
Fairchild Mountain. Moonlight
makes a mosque of the rocks.

Yellow aspen splash in dark green
spruce and pine. Gullies where streams
slash during spring snowmelt.

One rock, feather or flower worth
more than money. Need no wallet,
keys. Just clothes for fur.

All day climb toward saddle to see
what's on other side. One hawk floating
among bare peaks and over valleys.

Wind at 13,000 feet
turns to sleet. Turn back from peak,
take boulders two at a time down.

Winter moves into mountains.
Then we fly from Denver to New York
where it's still summer.

Early and Late Autumn

Picture yourself this summer
sleeves rolled, tie loose
free among cafes

late sunset, long avenue
a strolling memory
of seasons, love and loneliness

you get home
open window
crickets' song

and lie down with nothing on
a breeze softly
sways the maps against the wall

        ★   ★   ★

Three a.m.
    November moon
        The last faint cricket.

The Terminator

One leaf falls
holographic illusion
across time the Terminator travels
to shape Sarah Connors' destiny.
Heart attack
a common enough destiny
as common as young men discussing girls' tits.
The Constitution
is the document we refer to, the lodestone
to correct course and not go crazily astray.
Lose all purpose beyond murder, child sex and food hording.
Illuminated manuscripts
in a dark age, tape decks remind us of our voice
our communal voice
Supremes and Fred Astaire
the silken wail.

I lie alone in the night
its sensuality makes the best sense
it does or does not clarify the day
of classes or clients or chain saws
whatever fever may have infected me at the moment
a fever to achieve access to foreign films while living in the mountain
    community of Schroon Lake
the fever to instruct the American people how to apply ideals and
    practicalities of Constitution to international relationships
the fever not to die today, to maintain consciousness just one more season
    (and one more after that).

Anyway, what is being discussed–
the finiteness of one life–
or perhaps existence continues in another dimension, on another frequency
no owl hoots
but other purpler and indigo occurrences
with other purposes
as incomprehensible and wonderful as these purposes
to choke on a cherry pit or nuclear bomb
to wail our wail together

each individual identifiable hoot and wail, loud laugh and suppressed scream
one orbicular chant, humanity, from India to Indiana
complete, one sing.

I feel this way
searching for my place among you
childless, but a child among children
obeying or not obeying the speed limit
as my hormones permit
everywhere among brothers, the sisters among sisters
the races together exterminating the last rhinoceros and preserving its
        genes at the zoological society
my species attacking entire rain forests, temperate forests and boreal forests
like the engraver beetle in the red pine's inner bark.
Thus, I occasionally cheer the Terminator
cheer the machine and neutron bomb
even in the face of individual heroics, the male and female face
their physical love, tender and violent
I don't know what I want.

It could be simple
as this headache.
Not to despair
just to care enough to think clearly and accept 10,000 years of history.
Not to hate those in authority
humor is the only remedy
yellow ape teeth chimping in the glass death face
and ritual is remedy
a death song
and one for planting
and one for the beginning of loving.

Cities in Flight

In *Cities in Flight*
transformations are chronicled over generations.
It can make us cry
out for the genius occurring
now and in our past. How
the unseen, unknown participant
was made known to himself
through devotion to those outside himself. He
guides his city
into space.

So, the father and the teacher
guide the family and the student
through the close spaces of knowledge
and obligation. And perform
the history that surrounds them.
Good actors and directors,
philosophers and physicists,
soldiers and foresters.

Today
steam rose from the asphalt
because the sun
has arrived in place, powerful, equinoxal
as the human song
that receives it.

Two big deer
    Lope cautiously
        Off the open road.

Two crows
    Fly low
        Above the Oswegatchie.

Frank Bassett
forester since '57
marks a stand of maple and black cherry

for selective cutting. His actions today
will be noted
by another forester, also acting alone,
in the 21st century.

New York City
in a froth of creativity
Pacino and Sheen in Julius Caesar,
Sonny Rollins at Town Hall,
films opening, one
that portrays the flamboyant style
and dedication
of a barrio public school teacher.

You cannot act alone.
You must belong
in your heart
to the flight humanity makes in Spring, north
toward wild flowers
in geese chevrons.

Upside Down the Ancient Bole

The white-breasted nuthatch
upside down the ancient bole.
If it has no soul, neither do I.

Pencils criss-crossed on the desk,
sticks tangled on the ground.
Oblong lenticels, yellow stars.

We try to worship the divine
in our sexual partners. They shit and sweat diurnally
and fear their deaths. But the abstract

God has also died. He lied to say he was
eternal. Earth must burn, universe grow cold.
Old field species become ornamentals.

Mosquitoes prey on us, and black flies.
The body decays, and this is what you come
to love. And the ants that carry it away.

This morning, the profusion of species
contents me. The temperate zone is warm, late May.
The posture of that bird is good to emulate.

Silence of winter

Silence of winter
distant from all but my sexual contacts
her bedroom nights
and day friends
memory of my independence vanishing dream
holding on to it, myself
knowing how love can hurt.

Its seduction of me, dissolving my man barriers
biologically, to procreate
or create a new personality, a deepening
humility, her womanhood hands.
Not giving in completely
touching sweetly
but staying strong.

Going into the winter to mark my trees
not flinching in the dark early morning
casting an eye cold as a telescope
moving inexorably
a part of nature, insect, star.
This is how I'll love
and live with her.

Late Summer

It has been beautiful, late August, full moon
a million crickets following
a million fireflies in June,
a million May peepers. Immersed
in insect, amphibian cycles, I am a mammal, drugged,
crossing the road, car approaching
fast, unnoticed.

I would choose to die in late summer.
Why?
So that my wife would have autumn, intense,
to grieve by,
snowy bandages with which to bind the wound,
and spring to reawaken into.
Summer to remember that she's loved.

To identify or classify

To identify or classify
birds by
the complexity or beauty
of their songs.

And so
what is over that
ridge or hill
a sink-hole, a sand dune, a steep bluff.

What must I do. Organize
the heretofore unorganized. The rabble
of unemployed child abusers.
Molesters of their intimates.

Are there dysfunctional bird families?
Simply put, they do not survive.
We have hope
that everyone alive is essential,

consequential. We classify
and specify.
The commonplace and everyday
is sanctified.

What happens everyday?
Morning is quiet, everyone at work.
Home writing, watching birds.
Afternoons, kids come back from school.

Evenings, watch tv.
Scotch and Star Trek.
Captain Picard's problems eclipse
ours who stayed behind.

So, what am I trying to do.
Organize the unemployed, the welfare mothers
and alcoholics
into a flying chevron of purposeful explorers?

Pokeweed waits

Pokeweed waits
underground, snow crusts
small greenish white flowers, leaves entire
and alternate, black berries
poisonous, ripe late.

Waits patiently past February
when the sun stays up in the sky more than January
and six more months after that
past the peepers keeping watch
for every passing dog or truck.

We await our time
or have had it, or are having it.
Body in slow, not precipitous, decline.
Expend ourselves on work and wine.
Percent of budget expended, year to date.

I heard a redwing this morning
who might have been choosing a nest site
holding the spot against chevrons from the south.
Choosing the best site, away from predators, near water,
in sight of seed and buds.

It happens that when the pokeweed fruit pokes out
the chicks were born, the fledglings flown
leaves already leathery
and the weather has the faintest
hint of January's cold snow hold.

Cosmo's Moon

The only problem with Moonstruck
is Cosmo's moon could never be so large in winter,
stand for luck.

Mid-winter sledding brought joy
snow, speed, although the kids were beautiful
none were boys.

Walking the boundaries, and the old field
boundaries. Aged maples, barbed wire
past the cambium.

Northern hardwood all the way, except
less than an acre scotch pine plantation
and a few primeval spruce.

Pendant spruce cones in tree tops
colonizing the old field too. Conifers
a primitive civilization.

Lyonia has red, scaleless buds.
Shrub or small tree, maximum height 12 feet.
It's a heath, Ericaceae.

Small, white, bell-like flowers become
seamed capsules, similar to but smaller than
laurel, Kalmia.

The buds had me thinking red chokeberry,
Rosaceae, but of course the fruit
was completely wrong for a rose.

A timber stand improvement now
in the scotch pine would encourage tall
even straight trees, a cathedral.

The maples on the upper rocky slopes
where the skidders couldn't or wouldn't go

are impressive as eagles', hawks' nests.

Mid-summer, Spiraea, field of pink flowers
fully encircled by mountain ranges.
Bees working them.

Nancy, the broker, coming at five.
These 160 acres, a dream, are unnecessary.
Offer 500 dollars per acre.

Not an investment, a sanctuary.
Backed against the Taconic ridge,
real moon rising.

Blackbrush

Blackbrush — Coleogyne ramosissima
the dominant understory shrub
in the pinyon-juniper canyons.

Mountain-mahogany — Cercocarpus montanus and ledifolia.
Single-leaf ash — Fraxinus anomalus
and possibly a western hophornbeam

by the small birch-like leaves
and the shredding bark
in a moist stretch of joint trail.

The joint-fir, green ephedra
looks like an ocean plant.
Could the wind or white water rivers alone

have shaped these sandstone, red rock forms?
Network of canyons, inverse of mountains.
It had to be ocean

ebbing and flowing, emotionally, like wind,
moving atmosphere, thicker
shaving, scraping, polishing, gouging, digging

fish canyons
then, shallower, dinosaur swamps
now, dry, rock gardens.

Explain the human history with water:
did the Anasazi visit neighbors
along the canyon rims and deep within,

combination caves and red-rock houses
small windows, doorways, just crawlways,
with corn gifts on summer evenings

when the canyon bottoms held permanent, not intermittent,
streams? After them

came the Ute and Navajo, Spanish and English.

Ravens dine on road kill.
A few long red roads connect some canyons.
The unprotected flats are overgrazed, rabbitbrush.

It is interesting
that as I learn the woody and herbaceous plants,
walk the desert foothills, I too could stay.

Grand Canyon

The Grand Canyon is like the brain
with deep, unexplored fissures and tributaries,
the main route well known by now.

I am walking, walking inside my mind,
a grand canyon, a planet of canyons, a system
of planets. The exploration may become dangerous

I might lose my job, forgetting to go or losing
sight of its importance. But the job is gathering
pinyon nuts and saguaro fruits, it is the main

river, deepest cavity, how I find the unexplored
canyons and tributaries of my neighbors
and my enemies. But is it a religion,

a reason for living. It is a marriage, for better
or worse, with all the other living. The concept
of life's brevity, temporary compared

with the time taken to carve the canyon, does
not interest me. Each moment has a weather,
is a mirror of all other moments. The naming

of things goes on. Cliff rose and wavyleaf oak,
new mexican locust and sagebrush among ponderosa
and pinyon pine, juniper. Once I know

who they are inhabiting the canyon, the raven's
flight is meaningful. The raven's rock cave,
search for seed and carrion, my home and job.

The Rwandan dead

News photo of the Rwandan dead
bobbing naked at the base
of waterfall. Wide hips and narrow
shoulders, surely a young woman once
sexually active. No solution
to death's finality. Peace
is a great blessing. Fools
worship war.

Is the production and distribution
of food and other essential services
fragile or deeply embedded.
Can or cannot the economy
support the growing or diminishing population.
The Road Warrior, however shallow,
attracts for its vision of social breakdown
and the sources of regeneration. Of course
Jane Jacobs is more complex and compelling.

The Rwandan dead
had dalliances and alliances.
It is the indignity of their exposure
and the rapid decay of their former lives.
How disposable, mere mulch, fertilizer
for wild vegetation.
Molecular bonds loosening
and joining new forms.

How do the vast darkness
extending to the ends of the expanding
universe and the temporal light of human
consciousness interact
to make the world?

What Have I Seen?

Sunrise, late winter
       skunk smell, turkey flock
            playful otter, too.

     ★   ★   ★

The white heron, a great blue,
     white phase,
          in the abandoned beaver pond.

     ★   ★   ★

Purple clematis
     its long-awned achenes in globose heads
          spidery, fiery, extravagant fruit!

Beautiful Girls

The search for a meaningful life
in a stable society ("Beautiful Girls") versus
the search for meaning in a war zone
("Men With Guns"). Finding and being found
by a woman, enjoying some romance, having
children and in that context earning a living
which becomes what you say when someone asks
what you do.

The doctor's conscious, organized, naive attempt
to do good, his legacy, versus the randomness
of the road and the war zone. There
his legacy is his rectitude and natural
rough compassion for the damaged people
he encounters. The difference
between planning a legacy as if you knew
enough to control events
and letting the legacy arise
from events themselves, controlling,
insofar as you are able, only
your own actions and reactions. The doctor's
leadership role such as it was grew out of
not his material possessions like the car
but his mission, his personal quest to find
the young doctors he had naively trained and sent
into the war zone where all died.

Not one beautiful girl doubted
happiness lay in locating a good man
with whom to raise children, not neglecting
the interstices of kindness, romance, gentleness,
perhaps even danger. The walls of the house
contain and define the small bubble
of warm air, surrounded today by winter
bright or summer rain
and that atmosphere in turn encompassed by
universal night and nuclear storms.

None of us are the men we thought
we would become and those of us who had
no thought of who we should become
are most willing to wage war
not even for the ideology, just the simplicity
of doing something that proves we are alive
since the outcome will so easily be the opposite.

Night Drive Home

Night drive home
no cars behind or ahead
the day had been satisfying
victories, compromises, achievements

half hour to home
bubble of warm air and light
moving toward it in my metal bubble
toward my wife and children

watch for patches of ice
casually, not nervously
maintaining velocity and analyzing
Jim Hall's and Paul Desmond's Bewitched

which way should I go
back west past industrialized cities
to spruce-fir forests
then what? the same

need for man-made implements,
refreshments, even names
they gave the rocks and trees.
Not one thing or thought uniquely mine.

Whether I am a visitor to my life
or the actual owner, inside
the bubble of air, water, blood
that must not now slide off the road

into time.

Bad Movie

We should have gone outside instead of watching one
of the sillier, senseless, meaningless movies it is possible
to rent or buy. Winter or not the fields and woods
are at least real, commensal and understandable if
you know the genus and species. Know the genome
and biome. Learn the physics and music.

But this much reality requires an escape, hence
bad movie. A bad book is better than a bad movie.
A good movie trumps a bad book, but a good book is best
and a great poem trumps all. Will my son Zach be one
who applies the scientific method? Can Aaron explain
God's intentions to the people? Their mother and I will wait.

New Mind

The mind is the body
paying attention to what
it is seeing and doing.

Morning tea, unemployed
was one thing twenty years ago
and another now, two babies.

Yet when the boys pay
attention to what they do
a small rift in time opens

to prepare myself to name
plants and play
tunes. In that rift

the quiet morning streams
by. Work on clothing,
tools and food

gathering and preparation.
The young children practice
holding hands steady

new mind to attend.

Sub-atomic particles

Sub-atomic particles
the atoms they form
molecules, cell organelles
cells, machinery of life
organs, organisms
communities and ecosystems
planets, solar systems, galaxies
galactic clusters and their inverse
black holes the doors to other
universes, a contradiction
in terms.
            For language and its shadow
consciousness must hold matter
the material world snugly inside concepts
theories and hypotheses to be
experimentally verified using vision
and the other senses, collecting data
and interpreting the known facts
accumulated over time.
                        Can matter
exist without a consciousness to behold it?

Believing in
our mortality (the species)
we have created God
(a supreme being)
probably not carbon-based
to encompass every universe
but is God
inside or outside
consciousness? Can God
tell us what to do
or must we tell God
alone
what to do?
            Here is ego
projecting personality, exerting force

on community, asserting the existence
and predominance of component DNA.
An already hackneyed theory that DNA
survival drives
procreation, personality, savings bonds
everything but poetry (most poems included).

Mustache, cowboy hat
horse whisperer, gulag master
Odysseus, King Lear
                        salvation in the details.
Yes, these personalities individual and interesting
as opossum, bear
oak and ash
beech nut, pine cone
Grand Canyon sandstone, Green Mountain granite.

Jones' Nose

Their unspoken opinions
are like a pot of unknowable, unnamed meats
including skunk parts
one morsel of filet mignon

Family or workplace
longer the hours, years of the living
opinions accumulate
perception strained through mortality

This stew of ethics
holds together, blows apart
trees, planets, atoms, galaxies
on or about year 2000

One must not
express the certainty
that the child's coma-induced vision of a dead grandparent
did not actually happen in heaven

One must feign
respect for all beliefs however abjectly
death denying
because they are harmless as

ozone
zebra
xylophone
zygote

A
beautiful day follows
on Jones' Nose
ripe blueberries, black cherries

October Sky

The teacher dies having made her small contribution
to the colonization of other planets by motivating
a boy who would otherwise be a coal miner to become
a rocket engineer.
                    Throughout the nation teachers
are sending their prize pupils through the funnel
flask to produce technology from pure science.
The mother and father are good, disciplined, god-
fearing people who stand firm against dissolution
and chaos. They hold their clod of soil in place
and others do the same to create the landscape
of community.
                    Communities across the nation
and the world produce the many to support the few
who make the tools and do the math to colonize
the planets. Once the secret of warp speed is
discovered, expansion of the species is
limitless.
                    Perhaps learning Sidewinder, playing it
imperfectly, is not a direct contribution to destiny.
What can I say. Please yourself. So
insignificant no one notices or cares. Yet
some stories may be told for centuries. Homer,
Shakespeare, Bible.
                    It takes constantly renewed
consciousness to persevere, retell the stories and
interpret lessons. You go, girl.

Engineers know

Engineers know
to build in redundancies
when lives depend
not necessarily exact replicas of the primary unit
but systems whose secondary function
is to carry the load when a primary system
fails.
      The principle applies
to all organisms and the inanimate
objects designed to support them.
But the sun
and the rock
that is earth
need no redundancies.
Burning, cooling
one
of each, they disintegrate
without feeling
for the mantle or the planets.

Some individuals
may, it turns out, be irreplaceable.
There is not always another girl singer
this one is the only one for us
at this time, while we're alive
in this place with the random weather.
The one singer, leader
the one who interprets God's words
when she is assassinated, terminated, released
we are not released, velocity
registers a mandatory, momentarily momentous
palpitation that is gone
unlike Shakespeare
so far. She
was not the sun.
But she was found
to be irreplaceable, unique
her song.

Let's work the problem

"Let's work the problem, people, let's not make things worse by guessing." —Apollo 13

I like his confidence, that working the problem
will certainly result in better outcomes than guessing.
A rationalist who does not depend on a higher power
to direct his decisions, but who may concede,
observe, realize and accept that he lacks the data
or the skills or tools to interpret data and these
decisions he leaves to his god.
                              But not before
thoroughly assessing the limits of his power. Guessing
before guessing is necessary makes things worse. The skills,
tools and experience are the accumulated wisdom
of earlier experts in his field.
                         Yet each generation
of communicants must examine the assumptions
from which the mathematics, logic, science or law
was derived. Rebuild the proofs from the simplest
truths, laws, physics. Taking God's first and only words
and extrapolating correctly, getting the trajectory
right for successful take off and re-entry.
                                 And then
to explain the derivations to your students.
Until they too can care for the species and the planet,
making whole sentences, formulas and melodies
from few words, numbers, notes.

To Go On

If you see a hawk
on a bough at field's edge
beyond the corner you should have turned
maybe it's a sign to go on.

Such as during an improvisation on
Flamingo or I've Got You Under My Skin
you play in the wrong key or mode completely
maybe it's a sign to go on, in the wrong key.

Or when my sons cry not wanting
to be alone, I'm upstairs writing
or just enjoying trees in every direction
it too may be a sign to go on alone.

Black-capped Chickadees

Having not done the things I wanted to do
and the things I've done not being what I wanted to do
I sit here looking at lichen on the north side of trees.

Black-capped chickadees
cheerful and truthful expression
grouped in platoons, sharing the point.

The tribes travel together
first finches, then chickadees
following the squirrels every morning.

What luxury, abundance! Handful after handful
of grass seed thrown, into wind.
The corn ripe and the rye with it.

The other main families: pines, roses, peas,
lilies, daisies, heath, birch and oak.
Maple, honeysuckle, pink, mustard, cypress, mint, olive, buckwheat, primrose,
     willow, buttercup, saxifrage, snapdragon, cactus.

Truth may be ascertained by considering
the truth we feel, the truth we're told,
the truth we reason, and the truth we've seen.

It is so good to be a chickadee.
To tell the truth cheerfully and joyfully.
In a way that makes others want to live.

To Fail Well

Fowl meadow grass–Glyceria striata–the striations
on the lemma. Drooping rachis
a weeping willow of a grass.

Recurring periwinkles, myrtle, Vinca.
Helicopter petals. Evergreen leaves.
Escaped from gardens, alien or native?

A little further by the spruce stand
a new mustard, cuckoo flower–Cardamine–
with pinnately compound leaves. What a find!

A good day turns bad.
After you've died, one of them dogs digs up your grave.
You may sit in the rain and think.

Maiden pink.
The dark circle inside the flower
a g-string or garter.

O to fail well. To lay low. To live long.
To run slow. Feel the hill. Pressing down.
Do less. Until one thing's done well.

Certain days

Certain days planned to be eventful
I look forward to for weeks, setting
and characters, and the work days march forward
toward the horrible or pleasurable
and the day comes, it comes without hesitating or hurrying
although I hurry and hesitate
and when it is here, going by
during my hesitation or hurry did I
think what I wanted to ask?

Belonging to the Loved Ones

To the gods

To the gods, the individual won't matter.
But we've said No to that. Here, you count.

Perhaps the gods, their tornadoes and weapons of mass terror
Are stronger than us. But we can read and count

And our music is more ethereal and real
Than theirs. They must divide to conquer us

But we have realized division is a form of multiplication
And have multiplied. Now there are too many

Of us to count. But we have learned there are
More planets in the universe than people on the planet.

A planet for each one. But we would rather stay
Together, continue to discover what we're living for.

Every man, and every animal, will count. And then
We will invite back even the gods themselves.

Family of Weasels

On last night's news I heard
of an engineer named K_____ who
invented the microchip and changed
our lives. How the chip now contains
a billion circuits which I still don't get
but what I do perceive is this engineer's
(a man modest in pride, fame and wealth)
achievement of Teilhard de Chardin's vision
of a world that is one organism and a single-
minded mankind.
                    Also mentioned
were Edison, the Wrights and Ford,
oddly not Einstein, Galileo, Copernicus, Newton,
Hamilton or Jefferson, Christ or Buddha,
or the unknown gatherers and traders
who invented agriculture, money.
8,000 generations and each individual
an experiment gone well or wrong, a chance
to respond with love or grief to the universe's effort
to extinguish us.

Family of weasels, young ones playful.
One reference says they're vicious murderers,
killing for sport. Absurd, I think, in the wild.
Another clarifies they eat ½ their body weight daily,
extremely active, high metabolism, hunt all their caloric needs
before eating. And, like the raccoon, ferocious defenders
of their young.

Ulzana's Raid

In *Ulzana's Raid,*
the Native- and European-American concepts of property ownership
     and rights
are incompatible and irresolvable. McIntosh
had no illusions about that. He said hating Apaches for killing whites
is like hating the desert for having no water.
I suspect the movie's not a good source of anthropological data
and overlooks the commonalities among human communities
to focus on just a few bold characters
as all art must.

I consider McIntosh fortunate
to have died commensurate with the way he lived his life,
rolling a last cigarette, nothing between him and the desert,
and no gravediggers waiting, jesting, defecating. Also,
he is lucky to have had one last, respectful friend
to whom there is nothing left to say. How will that be,
Kah-ti-nay?

Last night's performance of *Beauty and the Beast*
may have been the most victorious, ecstatic, cohesive
moment in our little school's history. Emily was Beauty, a filament
     of energy
who doesn't like to be touched and has been known to punch
boys hard. She had memorized her lines until she was hardly
Emily but only Beauty in a blue dress unselfconsciously
hiking up her tights between the Beast's advances.
Is this done in every American town and the world
over so there's no need to feel lost or lonely
ever?

There is no context for a man
outside the platoon or raiding party, home or shop.
When violence comes to the neighborhood,
the hierarchy of communicants will hold or fold
it is then the peace work proves relevant. I noticed McIntosh,
grizzled as he was, accepted the given hierarchy, a raw lieutenant's orders,
as he did the desert and Apaches, with a shrug and foreknowledge

of the outcome. If there's anywhere with no Emily or Beauty
we should bring them such blessings at the point of a
gun. But there is no place without Emily, not
the least-known prison in deepest space as long
as we do not hate or hurt or shun
the Beast.

"The snail will get to Easter just as soon"

–title from a ballad by Eustace Deschamps

Faulkner's comment, I imagine him
tossing it off like Yogi Berra between games
of a doubleheader. The hero, the expert, the virtuoso
has no real control, is going to feel
unmitigated, unsparing forces, a mighty sun
swallowed by a black hole, coughed up into a big sky.
The past isn't dead. It isn't even past.

Versus Wayne Gretsky's formulation.
When I think of my death, I think of returning
the chemicals and microorganisms I borrowed.
If my plane goes down, when we hit the ground
fruits with names will be waiting–squawbush if
in the desert uplands, rose hips on a Vermont farm.
The past is skating to where the puck will be.

I realize I have a religion, a science fiction
the size of Jupiter which is, as these things go, small:
Chardin's theory unifying physical matter, rocks
and all sentient beings into one–here's the catch–
conscious organism. Having said that, why not claim
the same for the entire universe? Rock + DNA = soil.
The past isn't dead. It isn't even past.

These trees cannot feed me.
Self-sufficiency is relevant only in context of community, economy.
Every drug, every vitamin is wrung from plants,
tools and shelter are ore.
A tincture, infusion, decoction, a douche, a compress, poultice, a salve,
    a syrup.
A war president needs war.
The past is skating to where the puck will be.

5 a.m., first of Spring.
Robins still in flocks, not paired off. But crows
mating on the sky–two couples dating
a sign of luck, that Celtic god passing Peter talked about.

8,000 generations, I reach only to my grandparents
but history and the naming of things extend our vision.
The past isn't dead. It isn't even past.

I was handcuffed but not beaten. Humiliated but not insulted.
And when I came before the judge, he was uninterested
in vengeance or restitution. He had his own death before him,
probably. I keep wanting to go back
to before the big bang, reading books about the cosmos,
FLO, LUCA, the texture of reality, consciousness, God-seeking.
The past is skating to where the puck will be.

For the next 5-10 years my goals are: geographically
compact and contiguous Congressional districts, term limits
for Federal legislators and judges, election of the president
by direct popular vote, public financing, spending limits and free
air time for candidates, abolish UN vetoes, consent of the governed
before governments can sit in global councils.
The past isn't dead. It isn't even past.

No greater tragedy than the death of your children.
Yet you live on, eyes drained of color. Old,
you make plans. To know the names of every flower
in the temperate zone. Every bird by its song.
Just as you're about to reach your goal, a tipping point
comes along: a nuclear detonation or it gets too cold.
The past is skating to where the puck will be.

Occupied

As a boy, I'd find my father
sitting in the pitch dark living room,
cigarette aglow, as I'd pass
from my bed to the bathroom.

Did the boy consider, at that late hour,
what plans or fears occupied the man?
Not at all, nor did the man share
with the passing boy what he thought.

Now he's gone. Back from that piss
and many another, I can well imagine
the mystery I must be to my son.
Has much changed but the date and where the man fought?

Most men, most times, abide in peace,
leastwise not always angry or afraid
they cannot save their children from the gas
or the abyss about which God lied.

Yet, when the boy comes through the room
in the movement of his body there's a sleepiness
to make the man cry for himself, his father
and the boy who'll soon sit in the dark occupied.

Every Other Can

–from a poem by Robert Sward

Anthology of poems, big jazz band
aren't dancers beautiful as boats in a fog? Muscular
and sweaty, stubble in their armpits, and pubic hair.
Smelly as fish in a net. O it is good, fit
wherever you go, as Buddha said, the clarity of your own dream follows.
    With a bitch
at every other can.

My dream is passing into fog-covered land.
Hard as I struggle to make the committee work significant
I am only passing time until my time is spent. Abstinent
but cognizant, so cognizant, of Dawn's body
from her knees to her whirlwind hair, smooth tan skin, even her feet
    which are like a man's. A lady
I will love if I can.

Everything I try to do is sand,
a laughing leaf in a joking wind. Our particular war
forgotten on CNN, in a file cabinet with old car parts,
baseball cards, the instrument your dad played
(he wasn't Pan), chickadees, woodpeckers, flycatchers, catbirds, Spring!,
    the kids' training potty before they
learned to use the can.

I've got lists of things I've done and
lists of things I never did but they don't matter, do they? Right.
Singularly unhandsome, I can give a fright,
but I'm amazed at beauty hiding in plain sight.
The cranky saxophone, creaky trumpet section, ham-fisted drummer or
    the wild edibles I'm bending over, tasting. Such dreams shall sustain me
    when my coffin lid's on tight
and I'm living in a can.

Avoiding beautiful September

1

The personal is boring
as are my ruminations on the war.
What I need to do I can't try:
wander without shelter in the backcountry.
Or go deeper into the polity,
join a committee or a party.

Minute by minute and season to season
I like my life but what does it add up to, what reason
to go on? No better than a squirrel
or a spider. Spreadsheets, fake books, girls
I want too mildly, modestly or morally to have.
Can the economy and community be called love?

You can be killed and buried in gravel
Your children can be failed at school and marched to war
You can be taxed and sent to gaol for the honor of it
And there's nothing you can do about it.
Will we find the universe not large enough to hold us?
Will planet after planet be too old for us?

If you were president, what would your program be?
What one question is the key
to another's truth. How do you spend your money?
Do you believe in a god who can see
all and understand? Or is he
unable to care, a different species.

2

We take the long view
that as individuals drop
from sight, new enthusiasts
will associate. Legs
give out, lungs collapse,
but we do not let the circle lapse.

For every Aristotle
there are a million toddlers
who will advance no memorable
theories. But the mist
on trees and mountains,
sunrise over desert, are for

every merchant, traveler.
My sons will take on cares,
which toys are theirs,
as their parents grow
older. Slowness brings us
to our goal: do one thing well.

By that what is meant?
Don't be a dilettante.
Not having found the greatness
of a single, clear description,
definition, the greatness comes in
doing everyday what's known.

The Recent and Long Dead

November is sweet, sunshine through bare trees, dry brown and fungus-
     free leaves companionably visiting among the dead
as I did yesterday our town's small graveyard military dads who recently
     died lie under polished stones embossed with actual photos of them-
     selves and their wives flowers and plastic totems within a miniature
     picket fence overflowing with the emotions love and grieving of the
     living
beside or not far from simple wafer-thin old moss-covered stones on
     which I could not read the names.
Such peace I realized which may be found around any rock or tree has
     escaped me while I pursue my particular happiness and our particular war,
and such a blessing awaits me, too.

Much like living

It was with almost joy
that I watched at my father's
deathbed. His struggle
to let go
of his body and thoughts
was like being at a birth.

But now I'm not so sure.
Now that I'm back
with my life.
Unlike Marvin Bell
who will never, never
see his father again

I feel the man's presence
in every third thought
as one who went before.
Twice that Spring he said
Rob, I'm dying
but I failed to ask my question

What is it like?
He wouldn't have been able
to say. Not
because he didn't know.
Because it's so
much like living.

A Designer of Systems

"I design systems that allow people to do their best work regularly and predictably, instead of intermittently and by chance, and to produce outcomes in quantities large enough to make a difference in their communities."

1

I say I'm a designer of systems, plans
Man's
Parts that stand together, set in place to serve
Trees and planets, too, which are unplanned by us
The observant, wise man
Tries to understand
Name the parts, pistil and stamen
Rocks, eskars
Elements.

Winter is shuddering to an end, mud roads
Cardinal pairs
Robin flocks return that will soon pair off
Buds
Soils swell
Will I live to smell it again, learn the lobelias
Understand and name the parts
It ought to be a great comfort to be so insignificant
Go among weeds, a wind
Thinking to myself

One's never alone
A dichotomous key is needed, a book of twigs and fruits
Accumulated over time and generations
Without it mine would be a blank mind

To be blank but knowledgeable
Without any machinery
In a perfect silence
That is the definition of death for which we have only to wait
But in my panic last night I thought death's inert
Grace requires consciousness

Hold on long to the senses
At least a century, maybe more
A boy hanging upside down from a fence at sunset, counting clouds

2

Now we go to our daily practice
And chosen disciplines
Sustained by the satisfactions of being good men among our fellow men
Women
Choosing to do this and not that
With the finite days allotted us that at first seemed like a lot
They're now few
But the chickadee's life to the chick and the cankerworm moth's to the worm
Seem as long to them as ours to us
What question am I asking today
By now, past half a century, I should have chosen a discipline
And been satisfied

To be a war president one must have war
May you live in interesting times—wish or curse?
Squirrels, high in oaks,
Fiber, fat and protein in acorns
Strong runners, leapers, climbers
Should stay off the roads which some cannot avoid being where they're born
Natural selection is occurring
Those that look for machinery in motion
Hesitate or don't as needed before crossing
Live in larger numbers than those whose modus operandi's
Guessing
The ravens eat the fur and guts of bad guesses off the roads

I impose my own small order
Having chosen mountains over plains or shore
Go to my daily discipline
And estimate the motions of the seas and stars
Measuring my satisfactions by my children's satisfactions

Birding by Ear

The poem requires a mind
that finds meaning, even divination,
in language. Non-fiction,
up to academic standards, demands
evidence. Nothing less will do.
Most of us read fiction and this
needs a taste for action, motivation.

Lately, as have you, I have
thought about our war and its purpose,
motivation. But I have also closely
listened to the wood thrush, analyzed
its song like a tune by T.S. Monk
or J.S. Bach concerto. One belongs
to the loved ones and they ostracize us, too.

The robin, on the other hand, is never calm.
It is the flute-like tones, yes, but mostly
the patient, meditative clarity
of the thrush that enchants. One wants
to be that bird. How will we attain
calm clarity for the species Homo sapiens?
Through the discipline of asking questions.

A terrorist bombs, a dog barks,
we do not know their motivations.
Can I be content to be silent
while the evidence is sifted by the many
to a single answer. The World Trade Center
could have been a sacrifice, queen's sacrifice,
ending history for global governance.

Too much doing is the commonest of mortals' sins.
Peace has many faces,
the wood thrush in the canopy is one.
A word of praise here, an encouraging word there.
A wraith, a ghost against a fat man,
verbose, sure of the path, always hungry.
Nothing satisfies like the thrush's song.

"Stay together. Learn the flowers. Go light."

–title from lines by Gary Snyder

1

At peace perhaps too much
a fine Spring rain
we seek news from the desert or capitol
of those who have dedicated their lives to losing their lives for us
adventurers, ancient honor, land runners
this campaign a must to advance one's career
a war president needs war

2

Walking among
bush, insects, predators
the bushman with a staff
no knife or gun
knows
each plant, languages of mammals,
purposes of insects, placement of rocks

3

I've read about those remarkable souls who maintain self-control
among murderers and the unentertained multitude
who may have even spoken persuasively
at the right moment for speaking
and thus attracted a now unwanted immortality
there are only two ways you can tell
a bird of prey from a vision–humor and ritual

4

the Fedex gal
would be unlike taking off Emily Dickinson's clothes
over the counter perfume and spray paint hair
postman's shorts, black socks
a woman's legs are much like a man's
yet she too is beautiful, too beautiful, weekends
boating with her man

5

Suburbs, lawns, blankets
in a long, long nursery of babies
napping, old
and, I say this respectfully, blind
certain and uninterested
in motives more subtle than their immediate comfort
Who am I to complain?

6

Plants, poems: riches
our financial advisor doesn't count. Good and simple
a man as he is. Comes tousled
from early morning golf and puffy
from a late night fight or lovefest with his wife.
Inchworm
letting out its rope down an oak.

7

Late afternoon meeting
like the dry samara, achene or capsule surrounding a seed
how often have I tried to escape
my manhood, community, chamber of commerce
you cannot drive
the roads are theirs and the signs, perhaps
you can walk if you can name the plants and snakes and are willing to die

8

O happy family
there's some contentment in letting community and family decide
your place in it. Gatekeepers–
unconscious god, invisible hand, natural selection–
kind when refraining from violence
when not responding with force to the universe's effort
to extinguish them.

Eastern tent caterpillars

Mid-spring, skinny, black, blind
eastern tent caterpillars—
Malacosoma americanum—
falling from the cherry tree
leaning, human, over our deck.
Annoying. Mash and kick
them with my feet, continue
practicing or reading.

Three weeks later, reading
late at night. Heavy-bodied
black-eyed, reflexed antennae—
many hundreds of moths
crave the lamplight, some attaining
extinction through cracks
around the window screen. Annoying.
Until next morning, I look
up the name that has eluded me
all spring and early summer.

The single-minded moth and larval
colony—one small monophony.

America the seeing-eye dog

Policy or personal
questions? In the poem Two White Wines
a child adopted from Cambodia
is a thing of beauty, and so she is
as she showed herself to be yesterday. Lovely. However
the poet implies market, i.e. economic, forces brought her to America
when, as her parents know, it was war,
the sad Vietnam War or the War with America
as I think the Vietnamese remember it.

Honor and bravery
equal courage. Reed Whittemore's poem about
a photo of Viet Cong prisoners, stoic, defiant
under an American officer's boot
expresses admiration for the enemy. Then and now
a dangerous sentiment. Your fellow citizens, denizens
of convenience stores, even your family,
may come to see you as the enemy. Once ostracized, the other,
not belonging to the loved ones, you're not long for
this world of dew.

Tits and ass
Ken says, describes America's culture, not its poets
or jazz. What's worth fighting for?
Your land, your right to be stupid on your land.
Now there is one large land, one people
and many. The vote is a crude, monosyllabic grunt,
no way to express the subtle degrees of experience
our long lives represent. Thus,
it is good, when the family gathers, to talk,
each person speak
of what has been forgotten, forgiven and forgone.

Trading or taking
every family must be tithed or taxed.
Every man who finds his meaning in war
will be pained into wisdom and gentleness.
Who comes home

comes home to a future that bypassed the fighting, or did it?
The oil must be sold,
even Saddam or Osama cannot withhold it.
You can drink your quota of water
and still your heart can ache.

Empire or democracy
of nations? We can choose to be the reigning kings
between the last empire and the next
or we can implement a vision
of collective deliberation.
America the seeing-eye dog,
not America the junkyard dog.
Going question by question
toward predictable, transparent governance.
Example: How can a people become a nation
without resorting to violence or incurring violent reaction?

Courage

It takes some courage to eat a legume's fruit
knowing what is known of each poisonous part
of the locust (although the flowers may be frittered).

What's pushing up through the leaf litter
before the canopy is out, past the stone fence?
Wild lily-of-the-valley is my guess.

Of 140,000 soldiers, less than 1% have considered
the fruit of the desert surprisingly good and varied.
They have stayed and married women who are crows.

My own land is a land of wetlands but we too
have crows. We have waited and waited for this election
and now we're divided into just two factions.

If everyone votes and every vote's counted there will be
nothing for either faction to crow about. All will be
well with the republic and in the world what will be will be.

What responsibility does a citizen bear
for participating in a war, blowing the roofs
off houses, exposing the beds and clean-swept floors?

Warriors at the gate, you will not run,
you will not bargain. Dig in deep, feet
overhanging the abyss, protect your children.

I poured water into the dry vase of garden cultivars—
snapdragon, phlox, begonia, bluebell, mint—
and have they not rewarded me with their collective scent?

Providence

In disaster and war movies
the protagonist (Queen) and her immediate circle
are protected from anonymous death. They may die (one by one or
    all at once)
but someone at least grieves.
Or the audience is full of glee.

But in Star Wars (for instance)
what about the many hundreds of nameless, faceless soldiers
in body armor and visored helmets, or planetary citizens,
who fall by the dozens or more, like the leaves this rich fall. I think
no one thinks

how one of them may have had her first lover the night before
and one may be leaving behind two sons he read to last night
and loved with all his heart.
Neither belief in God nor being a god entertained
can explain or forgive this oversight.

Ah, how sweet
the film in which no actor dies or if they do
it's from their own disease or golden age.
People grieve for the soul that left
and celebrate the soul that flew.

I was in Providence for a conference,
a town I had thought insignificant, not a city to be considered
a city in flight. But that night they lit
one hundred bonfires in the river running up through the streets and the
    face of every girl and woman with her lover
by firelight was beautiful.

Had the city been nuked
by a terrorist or rogue nation I would not have minded dying there,
with them, that night. It is possible
to be several billion strong
and every homeless man with a singing voice belong.

At Basketball

Basketball stands for war or battle.
That's why I think about the players'
personalities, in my foxhole or squad.
Danny and Ben are fast and smart. Dan
especially can pass making him master
and commander. To defeat them as we did
is very satisfying. Ben's five year old son
is intelligent but distant. Disdains to answer
my question Why are you you?
                              But I'm not here
to catalogue the men's personalities.
I like them. But each of us has moved on
many times, when _____ suddenly died
the games went on with hardly a mention
and his name has since been forgotten.

But even this, absolute mortality
of not just our bodies but our names
and souls is not what I came
to talk about. Yesterday, between games,
I asked Joe how Molly his daughter likes
the high school. He mounted an impassioned
defense of reading as the indispensable skill
when I suggested math, the scientific method
and history are essential too.
                              Also between games
Bob diffidently asked why my kids are bald.
I was moved by the care he took to satisfy
his curiosity, concerned the subject might be
difficult. He's a political science teacher so
I took the opportunity to ask What ails
the republic? Of course I answered myself
wanting mostly to hear myself talk about Iraq
and how empire is self-correcting. For once I was amusing
I thought, treating the subject with a light touch
heretofore lacking.

But none of this is what I came to say.
A new guy, very big and strong, a
bulldozer under the boards with a good
outside shot if needed got into a dispute
with the other Bob who likes to tell people
what to do sometimes, about an offensive
foul Bob called which we almost never do.
The new guy said If you can't take it don't
play under the boards which is what I say
when I'm pissed and don't give a shit.
Bob said You've been pushing and shoving me
all day. I said He doesn't *want* to be
pushed and shoved which got a wry
smile out of Danny as I put the ball in play.

Home Schooling

November and April
when the trees are first bare and last naked
have become my favorite months. All the food eaten
except last rose hips and earliest leeks.
Leaves innocent
as dying men and infants.

Study one plant or animal each morning
before writing anything. All reading–
poetry or prose, truth or fiction–
classified the same, the distinguishing
characteristics being helpful or boring,
beautifully or indifferently written. Then

practice trumpet worried not at all about
my sound or perfection. Afternoon, my sons
return from school, math and (again)
reading, piano. Wednesdays we walk
observe plants and animals and record
our observations to identify and classify

later in the week. Nothing else special
need be done but stay alive.

Bright Mississippi

–title from a tune by Thelonius Monk

Cold, below zero. Winter begins tomorrow. Bill Moyers' lamentation
about the end of earth and the self-fulfilling prophecy of Revelations.
Both environmentalists and fundamentalists apparently believe these
are end times. I myself am not convinced. Such panic attacks
usually end with the victim surviving and feeling silly.
Although you never can be sure this one's not the real thing, history
and objective measurements can do a lot to calm one down.
But not enough. In the end you sweat it out and hang tough.
At the level of community, we stand together, form associations
of like-minded people. We meet in the meeting house,
argue and pray. Nevertheless, nothing can be done by the nation
unless done by each damned litterer, scientist and American Indian.
Not a one of us left out. Everywhere you turn you hear the singing.
I myself am in the place between Lapis Lazuli and Bright Mississippi.

The End of Faith

—ending with lines by James Taylor and Kenneth Rexroth

Two thoughts come to mind this morning. The deficiencies in our
    systems of governance—
local, global—
and the first two pages of The End of Faith in which he mistakes
    political (acts of war) for
religious acts,
but recognizes understanding the workings of the world is not the same
    as knowing
the unknowable.

Every new twinge provokes fear but what is there to fear? That one won't
live forever?
The year of a man is the day of an inchworm and 267 years on a slow-
cooking Venus.
A billion of anything is a lot unless it's the distance one must traverse to look
at God.

How much silence, or tinnitus, can you handle? A chipmunk cannot for
    long
stand still.
Once the twinge passes I'm off to the next task: building a constituency
    for this compassion,
that solution.
The dialogue starts with a question. To know the question is almost
    certainly to find
an answer.

Conflating questions is the commonest of logic errors. No negotiation
    unless the
violence ends.
Why not talk while we fight? We can always kill, torture or assassinate
between conversations.
Justice, or retribution if you want, can remain on the table even after we
achieve understanding.

Nature is my religion, I know no other, and community is my church.
The sacrament

is policy debate. I attend church everyday. Our jobs are hymns (the
   classifieds
a hymnal)
and payment for services rendered is sung praise and gratitude. Walking
   and talking
is prayer.

Strategies to limit or subvert discussion are the only evil. Violence
is one
but not by far the only one. What's the hurry to build a highway or free
a people?
The secret of life is enjoying the passage of time and time is the mercy
of eternity.

Of Judith and Inanna

For the accountant, the librarian, on this cold day
there is no revelation. He will go his own way
to the roar of the tinnitus in his ears.
About our war what is there to say. Yesterday
a flock of bluebirds was the only color in the woods.
Have they arrived too early for their good?
Of Judith and Inanna I have Korf's fears.

Inanna is generous, Judith is dangerous.
On each the wise elders depend for sustenance,
protection. Agriculture is sexual
and wars end when men remember cunnilingus.
To savor the young woman's thighs and the old one's food,
to water her womb and cut her wood.
Is this not what's real, the actual, the animal?

The women I have known were bluebirds and crows, such
nuthatches, cardinals, robins, an occasional thrush.
They did not consider their bodies holy,
they found my seduction easy. What good luck
on the bed, in the light of the land, in our youth.
Our enemy eventually becomes our brother,
his misery lifted by coming to her city.

Caterpillar fur

Spring and spring.
Clouds of maple.
Skies of pine.

Red in green.
Serviceberry understory.
Spring and spring.

Skunk cabbage spathe.
Black birch sap.
Poplar flowers.

Opossum tires.
Spring and spring.
Blackbird wing.

Wasps won't sting.
My father died.
Town meeting Monday.

Spring and spring.
Sing fuck you!
There's no down side.

Infinite willow.
Leaning oak.
Spring and spring.

Budding flame.
Budding thumb.
Cat claw.

Bird yolk.
Spring and spring.
Dandelion

Shoots. Arrowhead
Roots. Waterproof

Boots. Old bed young.

Spring and spring.
Rang and wrong.
Thank and thought.

Seed and sawn.
Wait and walk.
Spring and spring.

Infestation

Two years peeing in the same spot and still no clue
about the small tree with thorns in the bole
and opposite, entire leaves. Not Gleditsia. One thorn,
not three. Could it be privet?

Full of doubt. About survival of the species and my own.
A plague of tent caterpillars, more than an infestation,
an insurgency that has left the sky naked, bones revealed
trees knee deep in webbing.

Another way to look at it: The caterpillars have opened up
the understory. It's not a form of terrorism,
it's an opportunity for otherwise repressed species
to assert genetic relevance.

A scientist gets out among the ticks and webs, observes
the march of barberries up the watershed, mustards spread
in tire treads, and hidden among this mess of invasives,
a jalopy of a hunter's roost.

Beer cans are also diagnostic. Inwood Park,
dog poop and abandoned cars, yet a copper beech around which
Indians camped. The broken asphalt and Spanish language.
Humanity followed time there.

When I see a fox, a coyote or a bear, I think What Good Luck
to be made of clay and alive this year. If I saw a cougar
I would not know what to do. It would change my life,
like an archaic torso of Apollo.

Look for the silver lining. Walk on the sunny side of the street.
Count your blessings. Life goes on. A little better every day in every way.
You can't take it with you. It's only money. People who need people are
the luckiest beetles in the world.

Two Hawks Aloft

Two hawks aloft
crows anxious banding together
Carol Ott comes over to my house, likes the warm weather, November
a California Christmas and maybe species will change places to reflect that,
paints watercolor ornaments, gentle Jewish lady
how far from her past is she now? or is she quite aware just not talking
    about it now
I wonder what she thinks the solution to Israel-Palestine might be
ask her sitting around the pool next summer
almost always disappointed people haven't given the single state solution
    more thought
we discuss Thanksgiving, the cleaning and cooking before and the cleaning
    after, then the insane Christmas potlatch
deciduous trees have a special winter beauty, conifers among them.

"One Train May Hide Another"

--from a poem by Kenneth Koch

Easy to mistake water hemlock for wild carrot
and easy to miss democracy becoming orthodoxy.
How say? One train may hide another.
–Kenyan railway crossing warning.
Also, the prime directive from Star Trek:
not to reveal ourselves to species as yet
unaware of life from other planets.

Repeal U.N. vetoes. Roots like anise,
two or three summers ago, it was sweet
cicely I saw growing on an island
in the pond. Are we an isolated population
with nowhere to retreat from icy glaciers
or the heat of the day? Will the hydrogen economy
make the distances of space traversable?

Name the parts, and parts of parts, of plants.
That way, when walking from the ocean, up
the mossy river bottom, through the temperate
mountains, to find a sitting spot below the glacier
something occupies the mind. What constitutes
consent of the governed? Unmanned expeditions
are man's decision, the Saturn and Mars missions.

Kenneth Koch was my teacher.
He didn't notice me; I didn't respect him.
One train may hide another, wisely
he said. We observe and record our observations.
What cannot be seen or measured
cannot be revered. All know as well as
their names, one plant or planet or government

may hide another.

All Soft Feathers and Flight Muscles

In the intermediate zone between heaven and hell
opinions and complaints, after much moaning, may
come to be held in common.

The way a flock of chickadees
moves through the woods, cheerfully,
each bird taking a turn on point.

All meaning must be found, here, in the middle zone,
notwithstanding fears that rend and own us,
of dying unknown.

A Spring day
the flycatcher broke its neck against our bay window
nothing changed.

I buried it, somewhat reverently, in a shallow grave.
No differently, really, than I would a man
who'd died suddenly.

Who'd left footprints in the snow
which became wild lily-of-the-valley, running pine
then snow again in time.

After long enmity
Sally hugs me, asks if I've been happy.
A moment in a year.

February, the light is long, more direct.
It's meaningless, repetitious
but held dear.

The sweet child

Open new trails
out of the frail turbulence
of daily concerns. Indehiscent
morning, afternoon and night,
midnight to dawn.
In the meantime, in between
do one thing well. Or more
if you're a heron or bear.

I have yelled at Zach and others
in my devotion to perfection
and for what? His quiet,
dignified withdrawal
was corrective enough. His parent
learns slowly to go slowly
through life. And take
a minute to be gentle.

The term gentleman, perhaps effete
in some quarters is actually powerful
forgoing and forswearing
violence that could have been employed.
Choosing to hold
in reserve, for rare
encounters between equals
upper body strength and inner anger.

To see clearly
in the microscopic universe
love and patience. Withholding
judgment, certain retribution, maintaining
a calm acceptance of almost anything
that does not threaten life itself. And what of
war, the northwest, inexorable
demise. Let them wait on the sweet child.

The seasons inure us to loss

The seasons inure us to loss
whether a vote of confidence
or no confidence
we are neither more nor less

in our hearts and souls. We are still
whole, history
forgets our story
but immortalizes us, nothing is annulled.

Today's board vote affects my livelihood
how and what I hunt and gather
money, but not whether
I live or die. That's God's and luck's neighborhood.

I like capitalizing God
although I don't believe and can't imagine
an intelligence managing or wanting to manage
this interface of rock and flesh, fire and sod.

It comforts me to acknowledge
billions of my betters,
equals and the poor in letters
big and small. I have no vantage

from ridges I have been
Cercocarpus, rattlesnakes, dry and hot
places thought, worry, planning do not
stop. May they inure me to my end.

The perfect year

The perfect year,
two equal halves.
One with leaves
one without.
Forest thinning out.
Bring indoors
swing sets, pools, smiles, thoughts.

Having enough and not much else is a lot.
The transfer of funds is a loving gratitude for work well done.
Not self-sufficient unless self
is defined as family, community and nation.
The world.
Universe.
Thus,

I settle my haunches like a bear content, snug into coming winter.
House will be warm notwithstanding the Muslim-Judeo-Christian condition
not to mention the Hindu-Buddhist vortex.
Searching space
for an entity
to unite us as humanity.
Carbon-based, earthbound
meeting, understanding and absorbing
the clicking, algorithmic logic
of passionately computing species, insects, machines, bacteria.

A world moves only as fast as you think.
If it moves faster you're not thinking, you're it, dead, chemicals redistributed
in an ever more painless process.
What are my feelings exactly?
Systemic joy.
Lovely the logic
we have invented and applied
identifying, specifying, classifying.
It can keep you busy
counting, praying
while all the leaves are falling.

God is correction, feedback and bifurcation

Vivacious, practical, self-directed
Mary Bailey, nice body
it makes no sense that just because George
might never have been she suddenly becomes a shy,
homely, lonely librarian without a dog or god.
No, it did not fundamentally matter
whether George was born except to his mother. Potter
might have taken over but why should the morality
of a whole community decline? As for the ship
going down, if a butterfly in China had fluttered
right instead of left 10,000 years ago
the tragedy would have been entirely averted
in fact the whole war would not have happened!

I pleasure in and treasure
my insignificance. If only
I could be overlooked
by the planning board and IRS.

One false note gives the lie
to the whole premise. God died
but was elected posthumously to the Senate
as for the Big Bang theory, when it
supposedly happened what surrounded that
golf ball of matter and now what
occupies the time beyond the furthest edge of space?
My wife over dinner laughs, says Face

it, you'll never know so stop asking questions.
That is how we must make music, mindful of our extreme
limits, our politics, our complete dependence on the theme
of God as feedback, bifurcation and correction.

Organization man

Organization man. In the best sense
creating the environment in which experiments
can be savored and remembered.

Then there is the world of interlocked
organizations. A world of missions and contracts
finely tuned and binding.

Is the formation of associations
as instinctual as nesting and gestation?
A leader may be one who asks a question.

Or may be one imposing order.
Imposed through consensus and broad shoulders.
Waits, watches, acts his part.

I was impressed by the list of distinguished senators
from Vermont. He placed himself among men,
orators, imperfect, in history.

We march forward, imperfect in our justice
and compassion. Overriding logic with conscience
sometimes, not often, when it counts.

And mercy. A seemingly irrational, total
abnegation of the markets, rules of war, law.
Good to be so flawed.

Toy story

Bright and polite
kids. Deferential
squirrels. Leaders of
leaders. Each man
his own man
living with his mate.
The great and the small,
all, the state.
                    On the other hand,
you find yourself
no hawk
but stuck
in traffic. Lack of
spirit, spiritual identity,
not free or free
philosophically about
no freedom. Caught
no sign
of letting go.

One. Bo-Peep's
sure Woody
is her man, an answer
to the question why
be a toy? Buzz too
would do.
Two. The men at least
have missions
leading other toys
through risky situations
sprinkler weather
or just play,
cleaning schedule.

So it goes
not homosexual
not hetero.
Not defined

by circumstance
or genetic material.
Gone beyond
the creator
to an infinity
that contains
him and us and our
collective minds.
Question is
can it exist
without us?
Would it matter?
Yes, if
that damn squirrel
gets run over.

Until the fight is done

My confusion comes from too much doing. During the news
eating cheese and crackers, drinking wine, thinking the world
needs me.

Or the falling leaves, the days shorter but so much brighter.
How the cloud cover of the canopy has lifted to reveal
maybe God.

The longest continuous democracy may end in another theocracy.
A bunch of voodooists with their hocus pocus blessings
and understandings.

Bombs and poison. Grief. Chiseled, tearless face.
Chants gregorian. Her sad, clear, soulful missives from
the city.

Unbelievable acorn crop this year! Skate on them
like marbles. Last year was a maple year. The ash crop
significant, too.

But not the cherries. Or a single pear. Blackberries
held back too. Sure the towers were a violation, but they came to
hold community.

One stands not apart or alone but an individual within
his or her platoon. Committed to the mission and survival of
the platoon.

Fedex leaves a package. There is or is no anthrax
in it. It is our disappointment as Americans that the world cannot
be trusted.

Yes, New York is the enemy and brother of Kabul. How
does one reconcile those differing communities and be a non-
violent human?

With words. Wendell Berry's words. And service such as
the secretaries of state give, leaving when one's time and work
is done.

Staying in the diatonic. Agreeing first on rules of engagement.
Then engaging. Not stopping the fight or thought or song until the fight
is done.

Their Words

What would be the point, in this first winter snow, of going
back to several of the women whose bodies I have known
and wondering what they thought about all these intervening
years. Inevitably it is their children, illnesses and death.
Their art, their work, community. How their words
enter your ears and stay forever! Rib cage and knee.
How we lay on the beds in our youth and late afternoon light.

At no point will the snow and bare trees stop being
interesting to me. Seven loads of apples went into Jim Kelly's
cider press Saturday afternoon. A paragraph from Wendell
Berry's recent essay was read. Those who felt part of that place
were embraced. Fields of pumpkins, corn to the west
and east. But I remember winter nights hurrying under
elevated subway, Bronx. Alone, unknown, I did not exist.

The point being maybe now I don't exist anymore than in Afghanistan.
A land to be admired, like all lands. How lovely the harsh
mountains and deserts, indigenous plants and people, adapted
ungulates, carnivorous mammals. What is left of them after
10,000 years of human history. Much has been made of the snow
leopard, by Peter Mathiessen. The city of Kabul is understandable
using the very same analysis Jane Jacobs learned from New York City.

At this point I would have to overcome a deepening solitude,
the snow of it falling about my ears, to hear their cries and joys
and understand thanksgiving. Has my father gone to his grave
without saying his one essential thing? He has said it, said it
in war and in preparing boys for war, and in peace and his wife.
Have my lovers gone to their graves already or are they still
in life? I have heard a random, strange selection of their words.

Rereading

Rereading the poems of others
and my own. Community across
time and graves. What's left
exceeds in significance
one's last moment. Yet
his last moment must have been
exceedingly important
for the poet.

Nothing he did that day will seem meaningful.
While we prosecute the war
a pileated woodpecker and red squirrel
compete for sunflower seeds.
A winter slow
to assert itself.
I can still see my mother's father and his bowl
of filberts, almonds, walnuts
quiet weekday mornings.

Both grandfathers read sports
pages religiously. I don't know
if my grandmother who gave me the
anthology of, to date, dated
unreadable poems read poetry.
I remember my mother's mother spoke
rarely as an animal.

Writing but not knowing where I'm going
unlike Joan Didion justly
cannibalizing candidates
who didn't read the Constitution, Bill of Rights or
Federalist Papers. It's late,
I have not vacuumed or shopped for food.
Instead I reread
Phil Levine's Salami.

Gently unexpressed

Spring. Same plants, same order.
Monday morning, open for business.
Tractor-trailers, day care centers.
Every leaf that's coming out is out.

To tonight's town meeting I will go unprepared and foolish.
It's delicious, the unimportance of my feelings.
Even our particular war is small.
Europe had one last a century.

Hubble photos of events 13 billion years ago
Do not put me in mind of the species' insignificance.
Just the opposite having witnessed the universe's birth.
But birth from what preceding state? God again rears his hoary head.

Nelson Riddle's arrangement for Frank Sinatra's
I've Got You Under My Skin. When the trombone
Breaks away from the orchestra
Like an elephant in love.

They say one must let go and will let go,
That God will decide what tragedy you need.
Not every seed becomes a flower,
Not every branch breaks out like Edward Taylor's.

The November moth's the fall cankerworm–Alsophilia pometaria–
Slender-bodied, beige, beginning life as the well known inchworm.
How to accept that this could be my last spring.
Or does the body still know spring when it's put to rest?

Our War

On the question of whether
Iraq was a threat
I would say not
weapons of mass destruction having been
too broadly defined, well beyond
the nuclear bomb.
The administration, however, thought otherwise
and Congress duly authorized
deploying the military abroad.
If we believe this was a fatally flawed decision
then we must examine our own system of government
(electoral college, campaign finance, term limits, gerrymandering, two
    parties win all)
which may itself be
too flawed
for honest deliberation to beget wise decisions.

The other question, bringing by force
freedom to the oppressed
and genocidally attacked
raises the greatest possible issues for an international order
founded, following a world war,
to maintain the power of the victors.
Can America, like Washington (George),
refuse a throne?
What human rights are sacred natural law
to which sovereignty is secondary
and which the world will defend no matter where or when?
What constitutes consent of the governed
and will unelected leaders be given the same voice in the same councils
as the elected?
Who, among the nations, will give up the veto
and categorical claims to sovereignty
standing by the world's decisions, following deliberation,
even when they're wrong?

In our war
more children may have died
than would have
had Saddam died
of natural causes.
We can never know
because we're here.

Footprints

Healthy red fox, maybe a limp,
marks the lawn furniture; not that we have much lawn
mostly hardwood forest. Strong oaks
many punky but lovely red maples
that can break off in a wind, dangerous snags,
ash, some healthy, some not
lots of young sugar maple and old, old boles at the edge
and several black cherries, twisted, leaning
human, arms throwing a quenching shade.

Our "footprint" exceeds 500 square feet
but only one story. Each year since I'm fifty
watching fox and chickadee, snow and shade,
come and go. I must go as I came
perhaps not yet, perhaps now. To city streets
or burning forests or on a military mission, desert.
Always, with myself inside. Having had sons
who now have themselves, inside.

What can I teach, them or anyone? It is best
by far to learn together. The dialogue
starts with a question. Each day
begins with a question. To know the question
is almost certainly to find an answer.
The fox has his way, a single line of footprints.
The human way is to know the question.

We did not discuss the righteousness of war
at the dump, on the conservation commission or while playing basketball.
In a vast republic of prairies, cities and mountains
it cannot matter to convince a few friends of your certainty.
One can clamor, one of a million whelps this Spring
to leave a footprint in eternity.
I was struck that while the ancient Romans wrote of love
the ancient Britons wrote of war.
The Romans should have been perfecting their republic.
No god could do that work for them.

Belonging to the Loved Ones

Why make a sound or noise
or do anything to the page?
Unison playing from polyphony,
music evolves toward simplicity.

Gould's assertion that complexity,
NASA, is no more certain than a drunk in his city
weaving, heaving his guts into the gutter;
by any measure, evolution's favored bacteria.

Therefore, the earliest poem taking joy
in abundant crops and the lover's body,
2K B.C., followed by Yeats' Lapis Lazuli
offers the completest hope to us, easily,

for living this life without God's help
or even probability's. We meet
in the meeting house, argue and pray. We sit
with the dead who gave their genes to whelp

ourselves. Today, and then, the one question is
What is the polity's interest in the private soul?
Being free means belonging to the loved ones.
O the individual, alone, cannot be whole.

Governance evolves to democracy,
man accepting sole responsibility
for his thoughts, his wants, his words. Pure,
vibratoless genes from a polyphony of wars.

The Summer Noosphere

Wet nights, warm days are what we want in the summer noosphere.
Man's mind one with weather.
If this is true, life is good, or will be good.
Can I be encouraged that my sons will find mystery on the planet
as I did?

How sweet the slow spring! May already and the canopy not out yet.
Woods quiet all winter.
Now I can't distinguish the many bird songs from where I sit.
Red maple flowers and first sugar maple leaves are, to me, the Christ child
that's been coming.

The ancient poems and the new make the 1/10 inch of annual topsoil
from carbon dioxide loading.
As a humanist I want everyone pursuing happiness; as a naturalist
I sometimes pray for man's destruction. As a rationalist I admit
I lack data.

O to play slow and sure, even when the tune is fast. Inside an aquifer
of love for the audience.
Not to fear or even necessarily obey the changing wind's
direction. Being here I breathe and make the atmosphere as seen
from outer space.

The song of the world will often take you far from yourself. There
will be no self. How will you know yourself?
By knowing thyme and dandelion, the blue jay from the hawk,
the heron in its swamp, black cherries and the one pear at the junction
    of the trails.
They are yourself.

Two White Wines

Dinner with old friends:
salmon with red cabbage, asparagus, Caesar's salad, penne with broccoli,
    two white wines.
Jane Jacobs could analyze how it all got to our table
or even how their daughter came to us from Cambodia.
The economy or market bringing a thing of beauty, the farms, the trucks,
such comfort. The ancients knew this too
yet we are anxious about famine, genocide and nuclear war.
How can we organize (govern) ourselves to end self-imposed suffering?
That Quebec and Puerto Rico may secede peacefully at any time a
    majority chooses is a source of pride. Why not Kurds, Chechyns,
    Tibetans and Armenians?

Difficult to write a poem about it. At table, candlelight, we debate
or whine about the other side winning and making a mess
of our lives. The election could be stolen, tampering with voting
    machines,
what policy question does that possibility raise? War in Iraq,
school testing, prison population. Religion, the abyss surrounding the
little promontory life.

It'll all work out in the end. Go to your daily practice, be a good citizen.
Another failed effort to write what I mean. Such confusion, yet
two white wines.

Miniature Juniper

Although I hardly gave it a thought
I didn't really doubt
our miniature juniper, a bonsai,
would survive our desert vacation.
                              It likes the dry

air of our home, needs water
once a week at most and seems
meditative and active, both. While away
I rediscovered my love of agaves—
                         sotol and century

plant—met Mortonia and became
reacquainted with squawbush, its citrus
drupe which makes traveling the long horizon
of the desert uplands endurable.
                              Live oaks—emory,

wavyleaf—dominant and regally spaced
giving ground to mesquite only on the sere
sand flats. I counted and drew inflorescenses,
spikelets, florets, awns but grasses
                         remain a mystery

their microscopic parts. This year
I'll study, give them serious thought before
our Spring starts. The cactus wren was the one
bird I could be certain about. Sunsets
                         made me sorry

the desert is not my home. But the ocotilloes
flowered before we left and that made up
for the vicious attack of a hedgehog cactus.
Impressive, ponderosa pine and Arizona cypress
                         the canyon canopy

watered with snowmelt and along the high cliffs
limestone formations predating our arrival by
ten million years of weather. Newspapers
kept us aware humanity had not accomplished yet
                         the end of history

and that was fair. The planes were full of citizens
who no longer applaud upon landing. Snow flew,
not a pinyon pine or manzanita within two moons
on foot. On the dining room sideboard, waiting,
                         our miniature juniper.

This just a taste

Windmills (and the Quixote's 400th birthday)
    Calculus, measuring and predicting change
        Food plants of the Sonoran desert

This just a taste
    of the world's wonders
        complexities of governance.

Who owns these mountains,
    that desert? Neither
        the jack rabbit nor the jaguar.

Powerless but grateful.
    The planes descend
        discharging us to snow or saguaro.

When the hedgehog cactus attacked
    Zach's leg and he grabbed it with his naked hand
        there was that day a howling in the wilderness.

As commission chair, I have missed
    every deadline, failed to lead
        my town against the state and corporate turbines.

Ethnobotany
    agriculture
        genetic engineering

What are your feelings about power?
    If you were president
        what would your program be?

Okay Love

Dear Robert
        I'm enclosing the warranty
                for your shaver In case
anything should happen
        I've circled the address
                where to bring it

Dad still isn't feeling
        well and is going
                this week to the doctor I can't
imagine
        what can be wrong—
                but I'm really getting concerned

O!
        by the way
                did you mail
that letter
        to the bank
                I hope
so

Today
        we are going to a wake
                for Phyllis Spina.
She died
        on Saturday—
                acute leukemia.

Your brothers are fine
        they're off—
                Yom Kippur
All else is
        okay Love
                Mom

Building Fence

Sometimes we like to do something for the story
we'll tell afterwards. Buy a '58 Pontiac, climb
a mountain in the dark. Lamar tells dirty jokes
with class, knows how to wait awhile, bend
a syllable and enjoy the laughter. We continue

with our absurd work, building a fence miles long
waste of steel and strong straight lodgepole pine
but even I don't pine over it anymore. We're
self-acknowledged children, fence is play
and livelihood too, but something cheerful as sunshine

for all the death it costs. There is so much life
a little death doesn't matter. We stretch our muscles
the men feel like men, the women feel good too.
We stand around, watch a young rabbit one morning.

Election Day

This autumn morning with the birds waking up
and the leaves changing is Election Day. I meet
Jane Trichter on the downtown subway and discuss
Henry's upset. Her skin is soft especially her cheeks
and she is intelligent and sensitive. The subway riders
do not recognize their representative.

All day, at the office. I accomplish nothing substantive
but I keep the aides and interns working
and cheerful. On Tuesdays there is always a wave
of constituent complaints, by telephone. One woman's
Volkswagon is towed and the police break in
to get it out of gear. Do they have that right,
can they tow even though no sign said Tow Away Zone?

It is an interesting question but I try to avoid
answering it. The woman persists and succeeds
in committing me.

The people at the office want to bomb Iran. A few Americans
held hostage and therefore many innocent women and children
pay the postage. It may be good classical logic to hold responsible
the whole society for the acts of a few, however, then
I must begin to expect the bomb and the white cloud that waits.
Apocalyptic visions are popular again
but we are more likely to thrash the earth to within an inch of its life
than scorch it to charred rock.

Corner of Church and Chambers,
German tourist's language, accent repels me
although I wasn't alive 45 years ago
and many sweet, great Germans opposed the crazy Nazis
but lately I've read Primo Levi's *If Not Now, When?*,
seen William Holden in "The Counterfeit Traitor",
have followed the argument started by revisionists
who say the Nazi atrocities never happened.

War brought many shopkeepers, bookkeepers close to their earth,
weather, seasons, death.

I see daily life as low-intensity warfare
as my father, the World War II vet, did.
Off to work we go. What is war?
Population control, mother of invention, diversion
from the work of making life permanent.

Today is Election Day and because it's a day off
for most municipal employees, the City Hall area
has been quiet and easy to work in. Henry and Jane
hold a press conference on teenage alcoholism.
Leslie, the other aide, who I'd like to draw
the stockings and clothes off of and feel her whole body
with mine, goes home with her mother, leaving me
standing by my desk with my briefcase at the end
of Election Day.

Troy and Desanda

Learning disabled, hopelessly unemployed
Troy McBride can't write the address for his next interview.
Warehouse stock, 331 Tiffany Street, in the Bronx.
His girlfriend, Desanda Gaddy, also unemployed,
with one child by Troy. She's much brighter
but probably doesn't realize it. For one month
she worked an evening cashier job until her mother
refused to babysit at night. Wants to go out, live
her life, too. Desanda made numerous appointments
yesterday, can write and find the addresses o.k.

Troy has nowhere to live, has been crashing
with a woman in the Bronx. She's on public assistance,
they share the bed. How Troy reconciles this woman
with Desanda doesn't matter. Survival precedes love.
Troy can't meet the rent although she gives him
subway fare. He dresses well enough in the youthful
style, dark shirt, thin dark tie. At least no sneakers
or a stocking over his head. Smokes cigarettes
but so do a lot of people. Hedging bets on life.

Desanda is tolerant of Troy. Understands his
predicament. No stable home, no money. How
does she feel about her kid? At least she has
someone to love her now. Troy forgets
to record the names and phone numbers of companies
he applies at. Burned out on angel dust. Wants
a job that pays and offers benefits. Too old
and desperate for a work experience/basic education
program. Needs a living wage, not a stipend.
But can't read or write or even speak coherently.

Interestingly he's not desperate enough to work fast food
at age 22. So the woman on public assistance is
a surer source of income than we think. Good.
Security guard may be the way to go with Troy.
No police record, requires no writing skills, just
stand there and be big. A job with no security

for the guard. Troy's mother threw him out
four years ago, although she helps out now and then.
He dropped out of high school in the tenth grade
kicked around the house and streets two years
doing drugs and partying. Met Desanda, got her pregnant.

Does Desanda have a contraceptive in place?
We don't know. As employment counselors, is that
our business? Only if Desanda brings it up. On
the bulletin board there's plenty of information
about family planning clinics. When she lost that
cashier job, I was completely frustrated, but not Desanda.
Takes it all in stride. I gotta admire her cheerfulness,
but why shouldn't she be happy? She has friends, family,
a community such as East Harlem is, not the worst,
and a purpose for living and acting in her kid.
She feeds the baby, negotiates living space with her mother.

Troy and Desanda wake up, late August morning,
hot and humid New York City. They have interviews
planned as well as personal business and pleasures
today. They have responsibilities, society puts
survival on them, never mind their disadvantages.
It is tough and it is good. Desanda will land
another cashier position, maybe today. Troy
will go for security jobs, I figured it out, the
uniform will make him feel better, the check
too. The work boring, easy, slow, perhaps fulfilling.

The dead woman's cat

The dead woman's cat in the furrows of the garden
does not let herself be picked up
although hungry and thin after five days
with the dead woman and a night in the rain.
It has gone to join the other wild cats
among the junk in back of the house. To be outrageously
fucked. On my way to work I try to entice it
with false friendship, guilt that the dead woman is dead.

On my way home I buy a can of cat food
but can't find the cat. I let her go
to her fate. Later that night I try again
but there's a tom waiting in her place.

Maybe I could have saved her if I'd known
her husband died last week. Just maybe,
no more.
I ask the neighbors what happened to the kid.
The kid lives with her grandparents, they just used her for welfare.
I used to say
Somebody dies everyday, it's normal.
You live under the sky.
Your body has legs like an elk's when it's young
but now it gets old. Stay near the earth people
that's the way to grow old.

Dendrology

Surveying
northern autumn afternoon
Pitcherelli, ex-marine, body-builder,
Lussier, long-haired father of three dark-skinned children
and myself, sharp-edged loner, ex-lover of a fair share of women
are belly-laughing in the dying sun. Clouds.
The crew, among trees.
     Laughing
over recent visits to marvelous cities where
we could not keep ourselves from touching the terminal buds
of numerous exotic trees
and attracting ridicule of stylish girls and tame boyfriends.
Pitcherelli before the Albany bus station
shaking hands with a red pine planted thirty years ago.
Lussier, one hand in a child's hand and the other
feeling scabrous bark of urban woody plants.
Myself among partially shaved heads and leathery aromatic jackets
getting close to the hairy bud of an unidentified poplar or sycamore.
           People
laughed, but we laughed best
back on our mountain
under the blackening weather.

Life is not a curse

I'm not hard,
I'm scared.
I thought the cherry was the birch.
When the cloud cleared
I was still afraid.

At my best
I accept death
As a necessary search, wary
Of philosophies
That assign us souls but not the trees.

Nonetheless
I want long life, yes,
I want to plant my seed and walk the wilderness.
But not yet.
First I must just sit.

Sit and feel the pain
That keeps me sane.
Eat my meal quietly and remain
A guest
In the body I know best.

This morning in the east
The sun rose on the lake. Again
I breathed. I was blessed
And thought to say
Life is not a curse.

The Canopy and Economy

Sun and traffic–day economy.
Six a.m. drive to plywood mill. Too tired
to be angry. Each day a step
toward death. What is being accomplished? The
small satisfactions
within each day. Book consciously read.
And frustrations. Package dropped, honey jar broke.

One of 175 soil types. With the fifty
tree species
comprising the canopy under which Eric and Lisa clean their baby's face.

Sun in winter, old apples.

Inside the school
a brilliant but rebellious history teacher
is suspended by the school board.
200 students
wearing armbands and painted teardrops
protest. Another 400
are silent.

Within each structure
human dramas and routines.
Nancy will not love
any man who cannot do as many push-ups as she.

Trees grow,
porcupine scat in snow.

No job,
no niche,
no existence.
How you earn money is who you are. You are
what you do to get food to eat
and shelter from the winter, summer heat.

Each morning I seek God
by holding still

waiting for the smoke to be black or white
coins heads or tails
wind dark or bright.

Flock of evening grosbeaks
nipping maple buds:
the sign I need.

★   ★   ★

Less need =
more wealth.
2/23/89. So much equipment just to sleep.
More than a bare floor.
Plumbing vs.
wash at stream, find a log in woods.
Implements of human existence
unlike the deer or bear who
nip buds, forage berries.
I cannot eat the gum out of balsam fir
or bark from a popple.

I am not Wendell Berry
with a wife, a farm, philosophy.
I like the accuracy
of counting pear thrips in maple buds.
8/bud = complete defoliation.
This insect has four wings fringed with hairs
and is minute, 2.5 millimeters.
Two species within the genus:
one with tubular abdominal segment,
the other with conical abdominal segment.
Sugar maple their preferred food.

All I need
are names.
Names and habitats.
Elements, products, decay fungi, egg masses.

Marriage, copulation, regeneration, education.
Machinery, accounting, hand tools, laboratory.
I need your names
and histories.
Sexual histories, books read, imaginings, unrequited loves, significant
    landscapes, broken bones, periods of boredom, favorite shows.

   ★   ★   ★

Immediately means
without mediation, intermediate moments
time in the middle.

Time in the middle
time in the middle.
I'm bummed I never saw a dinosaur, an ice age, a cave man, even
    missed the last world war.
Thanks to paleontology, geology, archaeology, history
mind equipped to take
time out of the middle.
It's in our DNA!

Why should she love me, her tenant?
Because I pay the rent on time.

   ★   ★   ★

Excellent. The white sun rose
and lit the frost.
Early February, late March, or in between.
Birds begin
discussing family. Sap starts to flow.
Where the borer spirals in, it comes out wet.
Birch or maple.

I watched from the window. Beautiful
but no desire to go out and touch
swelling buds of elderberry.

Is this shrub crazy? It knows what it knows
with elderberry knowledge.

Come Spring, so much to identify and name.
Insects, diseases and new flowers.
Lepidoptera, root rot, the pinks.
I think I might get married too
and watch the moons pass through the mists.

        ★   ★   ★

March rain.

Some snow remains
roads dangerous
but truck deliveries must be made.
                           The light
pushing back the dark.
Bark
getting softer, slippery
at the cambium. Sap
simmering. Summer
and spring are here and there
although only winter birds are in the air.
Some buds
break swell
want
to turn inside out
but wait
knowing better.

I too will not break or run
early
hold hope bound by ropes of discipline, experience
time the magic moments to come
take the last sleet and pain
slap in the face
glad for predictable seasons.

We anticipate however
drought, maple defoliation, increased gypsy moth infestations
which some attribute to our existence.
That may be true.
Or it may be that the universe
has reversed its decision on us
and there's nothing we can do.
But we will do
what we can
and some things we shouldn't
because that is human.

Continuing
into the space inside me
unconnected to the light switch, plumbing
fairly independent of materials beyond
food and sound.
Where I pray
like an oak
that the light will enter me
unbroken, forever
and I will live the meanings in the wind.
                                        Basic
necessities, wood
wine
and friends. And
the names
of everything
by which we know our way.

Pee Stops

Two pee stops
    During apple-blossom time.
        May–and damsel–flies.

      ★   ★   ★

How hard to write!
    Only 80 years to get it right,
        Identify the grasses, birds.

      ★   ★   ★

Do I covet my mother's piano?
    Not at all.
        The pictures on it of her grandsons.

      ★   ★   ★

Wynton says Practice 5 hours a day
    To be great. How true!
        But one hour will have to do.

      ★   ★   ★

Dad's last walk
    Past his tulip tree's
        Strong, straight bole.

      ★   ★   ★

I keep trying.
    If I fail in June
        I try in July.

      ★   ★   ★

The wind is empty of seed just now.
    Older, less is known.
        But so what!

Love and Death and Governance

Anyway, there is love and death and governance. With the birth of my sons, love was fulfilled. There is no romance left in love for me, women are another form of men. Perhaps their toes are painted rather than blood-encrusted, but blood runs from their bones, their eyes are friendly as camera lenses, muscles hungry. Death continues to be my every third thought, fittingly. Occasionally I feel strong, but when I don't it's death waiting. I think I know it's a waste of time to imagine being dead, as if being dead were a form of living. It's not, but last night I was reading about the efforts of astrobiologists to identify LUCA meaning Last Universal Common Ancestor and FLO, first living organism, and that gave me a calmer feeling.

Bringing me to governance, the subject of this book, how we manage together between birth and death. What can I say that hasn't already been said by Aristotle and Plato, the Republicans and Democrats, Hamilton and Jefferson. To start, your daily discipline is a personal governance. There are many ways to know a person: by their god, by their fears and appetites, by how they spend their money or organize their time. Who is in authority, who is in command here? On the other hand, leadership passes around and across the table as needed and the one in authority is not necessarily our leader.

I live in the Berkshires, a mountainous community about 140,000 strong. My irascible, aggressive temperament toward my fellow citizens has exiled or sidelined me to a peripheral almost insignificant role although when I arrived I was considered a problem solver, even a savior of the poor and the wealthy classes who feared for the future. Why mention this. He who knows patience knows peace. I have surely lost face often in my life. As a kid, lost most fights, as a man, chosen last to lead the squad or platoon. Only when every known leader had died did those in authority decide to use me. Someone must begin to write the federalist papers for the world. And, of course, it's being done and heard. Books in print, blogs, debates. My vision is a world where you can fly from Madagascar to Mississippi and be greeted by a sign that says Welcome to our land. Go about your business, setting off no bombs, and fly home. Perhaps take a lover for one afternoon.

The machine and the season are so far incompatible. The machine claims electrical problem. The house leaks from rain. The men who left the machine have started their own business. A new endeavor by which they will keep warm and purposeful. The junior partner, heavier, says the Grand Canyon's not so grand. Jaded individual or one to set himself against the depths, abyss? Man's systems. Man made the machine (and the town) from rocks mined next door. Some few men understand these invisible electrons moving the machine to perform. I still cannot imagine, i.e. my mind cannot move fast enough to know how so many particles can be sorted and split so quick to make words on a screen. My simplicity is terminal.

Today it is fall, early October. First day for long-sleeved shirts. The boys at school. I admonish Zach not to whine and complain about the work. Lately reading or practicing piano, prone to fits of frustration. To the point of claiming belly pain. Last night I dreamed I had pushed him to suicide. It is so important for a man to do no harm. This is what makes us crazy against Wolfowitz, willingness to kill to do good. Someone very sure of himself and shining, much wiser and more compassionate than me, has calculated for the world that more lives now for fewer later shall be sacrificed. The people he serves are cantankerous, disorderly, selfish and complaining. The same diverse, spoiled, unpatriotic revolutionaries as at the nation's beginning. Their refusal to be more than the sum of themselves is their saving grace.

Politics can be an escape from the personal, the debates are of little interest to a man in hospice. Will the machines do their work? How will we make decisions together? Roger Johnson's gravel pit must be killing his neighbors with the noise of boulders being pulverized to rock but Roger is certain his business is necessary for the public good. He knows he has a right to use his property as he sees fit. There is a noise ordinance, a state employee will travel out to measure the decibel level in your front yard as compared to the ambient noise level. There is a measurable amplitude beyond which the legislature has determined no citizen may be exposed or corporation go. It can be measured.

Measure for measure, all's well that ends well during a midsummer night's dream for the merry wives of Windsor. A million or more poets but only one Top Bard. How did he know so much about kings and fools and murderers? An Elizabethan and no Freedom of Information Act. Today it is fall. The legislature and president are at work and so are our machines. One by one and then in armies the leaves come down. It is not that someone must decide, *we* must decide how we will make decisions and where authority resides. What am I learning, sitting, watching the season turning? Content this morning to admire my sons' photos, reread my own poems searching for the prize answer, and answer the phone. I seem to be alienating potential business partners with a take it or leave it comme-ci comme-ça attitude. All you can do, the best that can be done is to go to your daily discipline. Driving home or waking up at night I think I'm dying. Do the much-admired writers of our time die more content than that?

War all the time. I've been fond of saying what distinguishes America is its daily low intensity warfare. Endless but not fatal conflict. Chambers of commerce, municipal government, big corporations wrestle nearly naked and will lie as needed for what? I tire like an 80 year old man of the storm and worry. I remember my early years when I had no known skill to offer and elections occurred without my vote being solicited. I noticed no harm or good I did was noticed. Autumn was all mine, mine alone, I was alone in the world with autumn. My mind could not stand it. I cried out for comfort, someone to obey. I needed to grow up and know money.

Anyway, what's this about, I'm not going anywhere, I chose to stay and hold my clod of soil in the landscape of community oh blah dah. I want like Shakespeare and other writers to discern the motivations of women, men, see through their lies to a humorous truth careless about success and able to explain why what happens today or on September 11th obtains. I was impressed by the critic who found that Shakespeare in Hamlet had tried to write about the thoughts of a man suspended between having decided to act and the act itself. Why bother he soliloquated why commit or submit to the great moment when mere men of bones and dust, disgusted with themselves and others are the actors of the moment, beheaders, rhymers, debtors. And, of course, the answer comes to one in the night like Chuang-tzu, or Lao, why not? The great moment is no greater than the small and the small no smaller than the great. You perform the history that surrounds you and go to your daily practice.

I'm something of a systems guy. I want the truth and death and worth to be independent of individual motives, paranoias, prejudice, peccadilloes, virginities, crucifixes, paradoxes, protons, protozoa or curses. I want pure human machinery, stainless steel, clear thinking, even handed, not a doubt that every doubt is wanted, needed, good to the last drop toward the ultimate ignition into outer space, colonization of diverse planets and immortality of the genome. Here's what's odd. While enduring ever more frequent panic attacks (and nudging toward survival and self-sufficiency my offspring) pounding and pinching my skin to stay sensate, maintain consciousness, I parabolate (always orbiting myself, eye on the tip of my penis) to another extreme, i.e. my belief mankind can escape the earth unlike Hamlet's dad's ghost.

A system is a set of inputs–values, policies, objectives, procedures, data–organized and repeated to generate significant quantities of desired outcomes without redesigning the system for each individual outcome. I design systems that allow people to do their best work regularly and predictably–instead of intermittently and by chance–and to produce outcomes in quantities large enough to make a difference in their communities. So I told Josh Rubenstein from Amnesty International at Ron Heifetz's daughter's coming of age party about my plan to reorganize the U.N. so only the democracies can vote and no nation has a veto. He said the world's not ready, with absolute certainty, knowledge and authority. I looked out the hotel window, this was shortly after 9/11, at dozens of American flags and a lone security guard. I'm always right I said to myself.

Just Us

Suppose there is no life in space, just us. And we inhabit Mars,
air condition Venus. Hold family barbecues, national holidays
on Mercury. Go to Jupiter for spas of ammonium nitrate.
And go farther afield in the galaxy and on to other galaxies
leaving behind map-faced men, crow-like women and open gates.

Who will be the first-born human on the moon? News
from the moon colony! And so on, on every planet where
we've visited and established dusty villages or vast cities
over thousands of centuries. Then, will we not have somewhere,
somehow, under some sun's rays become another species?

"Time is the Mercy of Eternity"

–from poems by Kenneth Rexroth, Tennyson and Longfellow

If they're lucky, everyone has lost
or will lose their parents. Dying
in the order in which we were born, more or less, is
one of the blessings life can offer.

Another, it is said, is work
which is the play of adults. Search
the Internet, any town or highway
and men and women are going at it, Monday to Friday.

Beauty is best found in Nature, whether
up your lady's legs or Tora Bora.
Deep crevices and an abyss, vastness, thundering cataract of Death,
Time is the Mercy of Eternity.

Born Again

If, as they say, the cells
of the body are replaced every seven
years, then I'm a new being
since my sons were newborn.
I have died and been reborn
neither better nor worse yet remembering
feeding them while dancing to Moment's
Notice, as they attended with new minds.

Having died, as such, I find I do not mind
quiet living with the purpose of a cell
unbound by minutes or moments
as men know them. There are seven
deadly sins, seven ways of remembering,
seven stages in which to have been or continue being.
None of them recur after one's reborn
and none are known to us from before we're born.

Of the two young people to whom I was born,
one has lately died. I do not so much mind.
Although I do not, he believed he'd be reborn
and who can say what happened to his soul or cells?
Perhaps in Christ we continue being,
or with some other deity, as the churches claim monotonously, momentously,
demonically and deviously. It seems about as relevant that seven
rhymes with heaven and rhyming's a mnemonic device (for remembering).

But remembering
what? To go to the daily discipline to which you were born?
I fought seven forest fires, took seven
lovers, my sons are seven, and my mind
is the sole owner and subsidiary of these memories and moments.
Unless I am to be reborn
they disappear with me. Masefield's poem continues to be
the most honest and chilling assessment of our souls' and cells'

disbursement. I can imagine stem cell
research may lead to a cure for dementia, loss of memory
about who you are and where you've been.
If one's not been born
this doesn't matter. But if you're being reborn,
in the sense of "he not busy being born is busy being reborn" (Dylan),
then it is best and most correct to consider your last moment
of a continuum with moments endless and entirely in your mind.

The mind is made of cells and moments, seven billion of them.
Remember to be born and reborn, early and often.

Can poetry matter

In the debate between accessible and difficult poems
Poets' poems and poems for people
Only the single poem and private reader matter

Both kinds and anything between can matter or not
Solid or made of air, a vase or heavy clay ashtray
One word repeated or many like a lei

An acquired taste, like wine, and like wine
Not sustenance, yet men die with their miseries
Uncut without it, news and mere matter

I advise everyone to keep a personal anthology of poems that matter
Or not. Perhaps it should be novels. Stones, insect wings,
Feathers, Birds you've seen, People loved.

Wetland Song

The April morning's quiet
and so is the November.
Wherever people outnumber trees
or the dominant cover type
is unquiet. Nothing wrong with that.
Walt got it right, and Jane Jacobs:
the city is an experienced,
used beauty. Her toes are long,
nails thick and hair thin. Yet
her kisses can be sweet; or
smell of shit. All my life I've tried to point my window toward
some narrow wedge of nature.
On Seaman Ave., over the roof
beyond the chimney to the park
where every dog was walked.
Could I survive soot and an air shaft now, pigeons and cats,
or even a desk in the legislature for my lot in life. How about
prison like Etheridge Knight,
Nazim Hikmet?
I've gotten soft.
When he builds that house in the pocket
wetland my window now looks out on,
the developer will have given me what I need.
Amphibian mortality,
gravel, fill,
oak, ash and maples felled. Good
to the last drop is our bitterness, our love.

Biography

Robert Ronnow has previously published two poetry collections: Janie Huzzie Bows (Barnwood Press, 1983) and Absolutely Smooth Mustard (Barnwood Press, 1985, originally published as "White Waits"). He has served as executive director of several non-profit social service and environmental organizations. He has also been a forest worker in the western and northeastern U.S. He plays jazz trumpet. He lived in New York City for twenty years before relocating to the Berkshires in western Massachusetts where he currently resides with his wife and two sons.